Winning Cooperation from Your Child!

DEVELOPMENTS IN CLINICAL PSYCHIATRY

A SERIES OF BOOKS EDITED BY
ANTHONY L. LaBRUZZA, M.D.

The books in this series address various facets of the role of psychiatry in the modern world.

Winning Cooperation from Your Child!

A COMPREHENSIVE METHOD TO STOP
DEFIANT AND AGGRESSIVE BEHAVIOR IN CHILDREN

Kenneth Wenning, Ph.D.

JASON ARONSON INC.
Northvale, New Jersey
London

This book is not intended to be a substitute for diagnosis, treatment, or professional care rendered by a qualified child mental health professional.

Production Editor: Elaine Lindenblatt

This book was set in 12 pt. Garamond Light by Alpha Graphics of Pittsfield, New Hampshire and printed and bound by Book-mart Press of North Bergen, New Jersey.

Library of Congress Cataloging-in-Publication Data

Wenning, Kenneth.
 Winning cooperation from your child! : a comprehensive method to
stop defiant and aggressive behavior in children / Kenneth Wenning.
  p. cm.
 Includes bibliographical references and index.
 ISBN 1-56821-733-1 (alk. paper)
 1. Problem children—Behavior modification. 2. Oppositional
defiant disorder in children. 3. Child rearing. 4. Parent and
child. I. Title.
HQ773.W45 1996
649'.153—dc20   95-20677

Manufactured in the United States of America. Jason Aronson Inc. offers books and cassettes. For information and catalog write to Jason Aronson Inc., 230 Livingston Street, Northvale, New Jersey 07647.

To my son
Daniel

Contents

Preface

Does this sound familiar? Your child ignores your directions, talks back to you, picks on and hits his brother or sister, and has started to tell lies. When angered he slams doors, breaks or throws things, and won't take no for an answer. You have tried reasoning with him, yelling, threatening, spanking, and other punishments, and instead of doing better he is becoming even more difficult. You feel worn out from the daily battles with your child and have started to think he is beyond your control.

Nothing seems to frustrate parents more than oppositional, defiant, and aggressive behavior in a child. Over the years many parents have been referred to me for consultation about such problems. Almost always, the most pressing question is "What can we do to make our child behave?" This is a question to which I have given much thought. This book reflects my attempt to provide parents with an answer.

The child management method described in this book is designed to promote cooperative, nonaggressive behavior in children 4 to 10 years of age. The techniques described have been used with children diagnosed with Oppositional Defiant Disorder, Conduct Disorder, and Attention Deficit Hyperactivity Disorder. The techniques also work well with children who do not carry a formal diagnosis but who are nonetheless difficult and uncooperative.

Throughout each chapter I have integrated my ideas with what I regard as some of the best child management techniques and psychological strategies developed by a number of mental health professionals. Most notably, I am indebted to Joseph Strayhorn, M.D., Michael Bernard, Ph.D., Marie Joyce, Ph.D., Russell Barkley, Ph.D., Albert Ellis, Ph.D., Phillip Kendall, Ph.D., Lauren Braswell, Ph.D., Alan Kazdin, Ph.D., Michael Breen, Ph.D., Thomas Altepeter, Ph.D., Rex Forehand, Ph.D., Robert McMahon, Ph.D., Charles Huber, Ph.D., and Leroy Baruth, Ed.D. Their writings have significantly increased my ability to help defiant children and their parents.

A number of colleagues have reviewed portions of this book and provided me with helpful feedback. For their help and encouragement I want to thank Leslie Pollack Wenning, MSW, Frank Ninivaggi, M.D., Jeff Summerville, MSW, Robert Koenig, Ph.D., Suzanne King,

MSW, Morris Wessel, M.D., Alan Kazdin, Ph.D., and Pramila Nathan, M.D. I also thank Toni Nixon and Anne Bauerdorf for their encouragement and Patricia Nann for her skill in preparing the manuscript. Finally I want to thank Chet Brodnicki, MSW, and the rest of the staff at the Clifford W. Beers Guidance Clinic in New Haven, CT. Our years of collaboration on behalf of children and families have helped me to develop many of the ideas discussed in this book.

1
Getting Ready
for Change

Environmental change is required to help oppositional children develop better behavioral habits. The goal of this chapter and Chapter 2 is to prepare you for change in methods of managing and helping your oppositional child. To prepare for change you need to (1) learn three facts about oppositional, defiant, and aggressive behavior in children; (2) conduct a review of problems known to decrease the effectiveness of the behavior modification techniques discussed in Chapters 3 through 7; (3) be aware of factors that sabotage or prevent change; (4) know the possible causes of oppositional/defiant behavior; and (5) learn four key social learning principles. This foundation of information is designed to be something like a "preflight" checklist for parents (see Table 1–1). If most of the following systems are "go," you will be well poised to begin using the specific child management and skill building methods in this book. Let's get started.

OPPOSITIONAL, DEFIANT, AND AGGRESSIVE BEHAVIOR IN CHILDREN

Fact #1—You can eliminate and reverse some of the possible causes of oppositional, defiant, and aggressive

TABLE 1–1. Parent "Preflight" Checklist

Review all of the topics on this page and note the ones you will need to start to improve upon before using the child management method in this book.

1. Commitment to child's need for help	9. Creating too many conflict points
2. Anger control	10. Time for yourself
3. Role model	11. Understanding child's feelings
4. Personal problem	12. Hectic week problem
5. Optimism about child's future	13. Fear of change
6. Blaming others	14. Not following a plan long enough
7. Playfulness with child	15. Causes of oppositional behavior
8. Procrastination	16. Nagging, threatening, screaming syndrome

Once you have started to make some headway in the areas you have identified, you are ready to move on. Be sure to review once again the four social learning principles discussed in Chapter 1.

behavior in children. Numerous factors contribute to the development of these behaviors. Inconsistent discipline, severe parental conflict, excessive punishment of the child, lack of parental supervision, inappropriate peer influence, angry adult role models, television violence, and difficult temperament in the child are just some of the suspected culprits. The good news, however, is that some of the factors that contribute to the development of oppositionality, defiance, and aggression in children are under parental control and can therefore be eliminated by parents if parents *choose* to do so.

Fact # 2—The symptoms of oppositionality, aggression, and defiant attitude are very durable over time. In other words, oppositional, defiant, and aggressive behavior in children generally does not go away on its own. Without parental—and in many cases professional—intervention, oppositional, defiant, and aggressive children are at risk for much more serious future adjustment problems. Reports of outcome studies show that many chronically oppositional children later become involved in drug and alcohol abuse, sexual promiscuity, stealing, fighting, truancy, dropping out of school, and poor work and marital adjustment (Breen and Altepeter 1990).

Fact #3—Even with treatment and/or a home-based behavioral recovery program, some oppositional children remain oppositional, defiant, and aggressive. If your child does not respond to the methods in this book, consult a child mental health professional to discuss the possibility of more intensive intervention for your child.

As a parent reading this book, you are obviously concerned about your child and his future. As you read the following pages, keep these two facts in mind: without some type of intervention, your child's problems may well become worse; and because you are in control of some of the factors that may contribute to oppositional, defiant, and aggressive behavior in your child, you are in a *powerful* position to help him or her develop better behavioral, social, and attitudinal skills. But you may have to make some changes first.

PARENTS HAVE TO CHANGE FIRST

After years of working with children and families, I have learned that certain types of parental problems seriously interfere with efforts to help oppositional children function better. For this reason I want you to review the following nine questions. If you think any of the issues discussed below is a problem for you, do whatever you can to start to eliminate the problem or problems *before* using the techniques in this book. If you are doing well in the following areas, you are ready to move on to Chapter 2.

1. *Is your child's need for help your highest priority?* You may feel insulted that I have asked you to consider how your child's need for help compares to other responsibilities. To be honest, I would rather risk your indignation than not ask the question. Take some time to review all of your current responsibilities and activities and, if necessary, reduce your commitments so that you have some time each day to work with your

child toward *real* behavioral improvement. If you haven't done so already, I recommend that you define your child's need for behavioral recovery as your highest priority and then act accordingly.

2. *Is your anger under control?* If you are an overly angry parent you will create four major problems for yourself. First, your child will resent you and will find ways of fighting back with passive–aggressive behavior or active rebellion and defiance. Second, you will feel guilty about the harsh way you are treating your child. Third, you will be acting like the worst boss you have ever had—the one who was irritable, abrupt, demanding, and angry! Thus your child's motivation or desire to do a good job for you will be *extremely* low. Finally, your child will likely feel both scared and very *powerful*, because some children view parental anger as *entertainment* even though it also frightens them. If you need help managing your anger, read one of the anger-reducing self-help books listed at the end of this book or consult a therapist. The techniques you will learn in later chapters will *not* work if you use them in anger.

3. *Are you a role model for your child?* Perhaps you already know that *all* of your behavior and your attitudes constitute the first and most impressive "road map" for living that your child will use to navigate through life. For this reason it is critically important that you model the behaviors and attitudes that you want your child to display. Thus, if you want your child to be more cooperative, tolerant, honest, patient, gentle, and

respectful, it is necessary for you to frequently display these behaviors and attitudes around your child. If your behavior does not match your stated expectations and rules, you will be sending mixed messages to your child. Children generally pay more attention to parental behavior than parental words. For example, I recently counseled a parent who demanded that her son stop swearing even though she (the mother) liberally used obscene language at home and believed that this was permissible for adults. In this case the boy identified with his mother's behavior rather than his mother's stated rule about swearing. Other examples of parents sending mixed messages include spanking children to stop them from hitting; screaming at children to stop them from yelling defiantly at others; and displaying dishonest ideas, behaviors, and attitudes and expecting children to be honest.

4. *Do you have a problem that needs treatment?* This is a sensitive but necessary question. Certain types of psychiatric problems are known to interfere with parental efforts to help children improve their behavior. Specifically, serious depression or anxiety, personality problems, attention deficit/hyperactivity disorder, temper problems, and/or drug and alcohol abuse are all likely to interfere with your ability to consistently use the techniques in this book. Intense conflict with your spouse or partner regarding child management strategies will also make the use of my approach less effective. If you think you may have a problem in one of

these areas, seek a comprehensive evaluation from a qualified mental health professional. Getting yourself help may be the best gift you could give yourself and your child.

5. *Are you optimistic about your child's future?* Hopefulness and optimism regarding your child's ability to show behavioral improvement are critical. An optimistic attitude tells your child that you know he or she has the potential to do better and that you expect improvement to occur at some point. By harnessing the power of positive thinking, you may be able to influence your child to live up to your positive vision of his future. Thus, under all circumstances tell yourself that your child will be able to do better with your continued support, encouragement, and teaching.

6. *Do you create too many conflict points with your child?* Parents who say "No, don't do that" too often create unnecessary conflict points with their children. Try to develop increased tolerance for some of your child's minor behavioral troubles and/or his natural tendency to get into things. Carefully pick and choose your battles with your child. The simple technique of reducing the number of times that you say "No" during the day reduces the number of conflict points you and your child will experience. This often leads to the feeling that things are improving already.

7. *Are you playful with your child?* Playfulness and humor are very important to the mental health needs of parents and children and to the overall quality of the

parent–child relationship. The more playful you can be with your child, the more likely it is that your child will want to cooperate with your rules and expectations. Good-natured humor, moderate doses of silliness, and a few belly laughs each day go a long way toward helping parents and children cope with those aspects of life that are really difficult.

8. *Do you have time for yourself?* Periodically you need to forget about children, bills, work, and all of life's hassles to refresh yourself. You will be less effective in managing your child if you are chronically worn out and irritable and do nothing but spend time in the trenches with children. Find a way to have some adult leisure time for yourself each day and each week. A stress-reduction plan for parents is an important aspect of my approach to helping oppositional children behave better.

9. *Do you know what your child is thinking and feeling right now?* Beneath the angry defiant attitude oppositional children often have strong feelings of sadness and worry. Read the following letter I have written for parents on behalf of some of the oppositional children I have known.

Dear Mom and Dad:

I am very sad and mixed up right now. There is too much conflict and anger in our home. I wish that each of you could find a way to be less angry and upset. I also wish that you could be nicer to each other. I know that I give you a hard time and

I wish I could stop, but often it's easier to stir up trouble than to think about how sad and worried I am about what is going on in our family. I don't think I can change until I see that you have changed and until it feels safe to change. All the anger makes it hard for me to talk about my behavior and my feelings. Please show me with your words and your actions how to constructively solve our problems and how to make our home a less angry place. If you can show me the way, I'll try real hard to improve my behavior and my attitude.

Love,
Your Child

Summary

Your use of the methods in this book will likely be more effective if (1) your child's recovery is your main priority; (2) your anger is under control; (3) you are modeling the behavior you want your child to display; (4) you get professional help for a problem you may have; (5) you remain optimistic about your child's future; (6) you reduce the total number of daily conflict points with your child; (7) you are playful with your child and use lots of good-natured humor; (8) you have a firm commitment to cutting through the stress in your life by creating some fun for yourself each week; and (9) you remember that underneath that defiant attitude your child is worried and sad. Now let's move on to consider factors that block change.

FACTORS THAT WORK AGAINST CHANGE

Change is not easy even under the best of circumstances. Below are five major factors that commonly sabotage parental efforts to implement an effective child management plan. If any of the following obstacles to change is potentially a problem for you, actively develop a plan to overcome it. Remember, your child's *future* is at stake!

1. *Procrastination*—Procrastination is the tendency to delay repeatedly or to continuously put off doing something until some future date—which never arrives! Procrastination is often based on the unhelpful idea that a task is simply too hard to start. When you say that something is too hard, you are really saying "impossibly hard," as if someone had just asked you to move Mount Rushmore from South Dakota to Texas. Rather than say it is too hard to start and maintain a new child management plan today, say: "It will be very hard for me to start today but *not too hard.*" If you can change your thinking in this way, you will be better able to fight procrastination. For further help in this area read one of the self-help books on procrastination that I have listed at the end of this book.

2. *The "hectic week" problem*—This is mainly a form of procrastination but it comes up so often in my practice that I want to discuss the issue separately. Many times after I start to train parents in the use of the techniques in this book, they fail to begin using them at

home or start to use them but stop because "it's been such a hectic week." If you find yourself letting your child management plan slide because you had a busy week, ask yourself "Is my child's recovery my main priority?" and "How will my child's behavior improve if I am not actively working with him each day toward that goal?" By excusing your failure to start and maintain the use of the techniques in this book on the basis of things being "hectic," you are procrastinating and/or have not made a decision to make your oppositional child's need for help your highest priority.

3. *Blaming approaches to problem solving*—Blaming your oppositional child or your child's other parent will get you nowhere fast in your search for solutions to your child's behavioral and attitudinal difficulties. Blaming others and demanding that others act differently really reflects your Godlike attempt to change others, which is something you do *not* have the power to do. Let others take responsibility for their own actions, and focus on how you can change yourself, which is something you *can* do. If you keep the "blame game" going, your family is likely to remain immersed in conflict, anger, and frustration.

Severe blaming also distorts your view of others. I've counseled parents who so blamed their child that they viewed the child as a "bad seed" or as a person who was simply "born to be bad." Sometimes a parent has a similar view of the child's other parent; for example, "His father is a rotten person." Your ability to search for solutions with other members of your family will be seriously compromised if you hang on to the irrational view that someone could be *all* bad. No human being is 100 percent bad!

A more helpful attitude to adopt is one of *unconditional* acceptance of yourself, your child's other parent, and your child as *fallible human beings* who will sometimes do things well and sometimes not so well (Ellis 1994). Also, rather than worry about who is to blame for your child's difficulties, try to focus more on how everyone in your family, *especially you*, can be part of the solution to helping your child function better.

4. *Fear of change*—Human beings have a great need for certainty and security. For this reason people sometimes prefer to hold on to the familiar, however unpleasant, rather than risk the uncertainty of change. If you find you are resisting or avoiding change in yourself or your family, ask yourself whether you might be fearful of change and why. If you can't answer this question, a consultation with a therapist might be helpful.

5. *Not following a child management plan long enough*—In my years of practice I have had many parents tell me they have tried every type of behavior modification technique with their child "and nothing works." Upon closer examination of why these techniques failed, I often discover that the parents stopped using them after a few days. In fact many of these so-called unhelpful techniques might actually have worked

if the parents had used them consistently for a long enough period of time! I typically recommend that parents try the methods in this book consistently for *12 weeks*. If at the end of a 12-week period you see no response in your child, it might be worth a return to the drawing board to develop a new strategy.

POSSIBLE CAUSES OF OPPOSITIONAL, DEFIANT, AND AGGRESSIVE BEHAVIOR IN CHILDREN

Another aspect of getting ready for environmental change involves developing some understanding of the causes of oppositional, defiant, and aggressive behavior in children. The following section outlines the major causes of these particular childhood problems.

1. *Failure to reward good behavior*—In families where problems have developed and a child is displaying oppositional/defiant/aggressive behavior, it is suspected that parents consistently fail to notice, praise, and reward (reinforce) the child's good behavior (Lewis 1991). The child therefore has little reason to display good behavior since he knows his parents will not respond to such behavior. It is also often the case in these families that parents angrily respond to the child's bad or inappropriate behavior. Thus oppositional, defiant, and aggressive behaviors become the means by which children gain some attention from their parents, even if it is negative attention.

2. *Failure to punish bad behavior*—Again, in families where serious problems have developed it is also suspected that parents consistently fail to punish in *appropriate ways* the child's bad (inappropriate) behavior (Lewis 1991). Thus children in these families receive no rewards for good behavior and very little appropriate punishment for bad behavior. The stage is then set for the child to display a range of unchallenged anti-social/oppositional behaviors that over time become entrenched bad habits.

3. *Overreliance on punishment*—Overreliance on punishment is an approach that creates many more problems than it solves. First of all, parents who use lots of punishment with their oppositional children often tell me that no punishment works, and they are absolutely right. Children who are under a barrage of parental punishment become immune to it because they have no way to escape such treatment. Also, whoever dishes out the most punishment in the family usually receives the most punishment from the child in return (Forehand and McMahon 1981). Furthermore, over-reliance on punishment trains the child to lie and to engage in sneaky behavior to avoid punishment. In families where overreliance on punishment is the main child management strategy, children begin to feel fearful of their parents and may actively avoid them. Finally, although overreliance on punishment may stop oppositional behavior today, it does not change the child's behavior in the long run. It also does not change

the child's motivation for misbehaving (Forehand and McMahon 1981).

4. *Failure to follow a plan consistently*—In some families parents alternate endlessly among starting, stopping, and changing their child management plan. Over time this lack of consistency can actually make the child's behavior problem worse. When you do not enforce the rules of your home consistently, your child learns that *sometimes* he can get away with things. In other words, his noncompliant behaviors receive "intermittent" or "periodic" reinforcement. Behaviors that are intermittently reinforced or rewarded ultimately become resistant to change. Each time you decide not to follow through with your rules, incentives, and penalties, you *strengthen* some of your child's oppositional behavior.

5. *Child temperament*—Studies show that children are born with different temperaments (Chess and Thomas 1991). Some children are born friendly, outgoing, flexible, and cooperative. Other children are difficult, rigid, and aggressive. Your child's temperament plays a role in how he or she behaves and how well he or she follows your rules. If you have a child who has a more "difficult" temperament, try to reinforce his strengths and any effort he makes to be cooperative. It is also important to remember that any child, however difficult, is a unique individual with preferences, desires, ideas, and feelings that require parental attention and support.

6. *Stress*—Stress can play an indirect role in perpetuating your child's behavior problems. When you are stressed out, you may be less likely to follow your chosen child management plan. When you let your plan slide, you intermittently *reinforce* your child's inappropriate behavior, which, again, strengthens the oppositional behaviors you would like your child to discard.

7. *The nagging, threatening, screaming/spanking syndrome*—This three-phase syndrome discussed by Barkley (1987) is common in families. The following description of each of these phases will show you how your nagging, threatening, screaming, and spanking keep you and your child in conflict and teach your child to be oppositional.

The nagging phase—The nagging phase begins when you give a command to your child, and he ignores you. You then repeat your command, four times, five times, ten to fifteen times. Sometimes, just to get you off his back, your child does what he is told.

IMPACT OF THIS INTERACTION ON YOU—Even though nagging mostly doesn't train your child to cooperate, you keep nagging because sometimes it works a little bit. In other words, your child's occasional cooperative response to nagging intermittently reinforces your use of this unhelpful technique. Your child is *training you* to nag!

IMPACT OF THIS INTERACTION ON YOUR CHILD—In those few seconds or minutes that your child is ignoring your nagging, he is learning that oppositional behavior pays off in two ways. The first payoff comes by avoiding a task that is probably not fun and requires effort, such as picking up toys or getting ready for bed. The second payoff comes in the form of buying a few more minutes of time with something that *is* fun, like watching television or playing with a toy. These two payoffs strengthen your child's oppositional behavior. Thus he or she continues to act in an oppositional manner when given a direction.

The threatening phase—Many times, oppositional children resist nagging completely. With mounting desperation parents then begin to threaten the child. The threatening phase begins when you again issue a command and threaten punishment if your child does not obey you. As long as your child ignores you, you continue to issue threats until you find the one that *coerces* him into doing what he was told or until you give up and walk away.

IMPACT OF THIS INTERACTION ON YOU—Like nagging, threats mostly do not teach children how to follow directions. But because threats work sometimes, you keep using them, sort of like the gambler who wins one bet out of a hundred and then endures another hundred losses for that one rare win. If and when you walk away from a confrontation with your child, *you reinforce in yourself* the unhelpful idea that you have no ability to influence your child to do better. When you think this way, it reflects that your child is training you to let him "do his own thing."

IMPACT OF THIS INTERACTION ON YOUR CHILD—During the time that your child is successfully ignoring your threats, he is again receiving the same double payoff for non-compliant/oppositional behavior, even if in the end he does what he is told. Thus in future situations he will continue to resist directions in the hope that he can gain some additional fun time and avoid an unpleasant task for as long as possible.

The screaming/spanking phase—When nagging and threatening do not work, parents often advance to screaming at the child or delivering a spanking to force the child to behave. The screaming/spanking phase begins when you again issue a command and your child ignores you or speaks disrespectfully to you. Out of frustration you angrily spank your child or scream at him; he may begin to cry and do what he was told or angrily fight back. You are now in a physical or verbal *fight* with your child!

IMPACT OF THIS INTERACTION ON YOU—At this point parents have generally lost control of their anger and are resorting to their superior *physical* strength to make the child follow directions or their superior *mental* strength to psychologically hurt the child for being so difficult. Again, because these unhelpful tactics some-times work at the moment, even though they do *not* change the child's behavior in the long run, parents continue to use them. The price you pay, however, is *guilt*.

IMPACT OF THIS INTERACTION ON YOUR CHILD—Being verbally abused or spanked by a parent will likely result in the child's secretly being fearful of the parent and his/her anger control problem. Children treated in this way also tend to use yelling and hitting as a means of solving problems. Remember, children learn more from their parents' behavior than from their parents' words.

Parents and children caught up in this vicious cycle quickly realize that the winner is whoever escalates the fastest to using loud, angry, and coercive behavior! In other words, in those moments when you are overly stressed you may decide to skip nagging and threatening and go right to spanking or screaming. Or, if your child is stressed or tired, he may decide to abandon ignoring you and stage a royal temper tantrum to get you to back off. Do what you can to prevent problems with your child from escalating in this unhelpful way. Remember, you need to take the lead as a role model for your child by demonstrating emotional and behavioral control when you and your child are in conflict.

You may now be wondering, "How do I break this cycle?" We'll get to that in Chapters 3 and 4. I will tell you at this point, however, that the way to end this dysfunctional interaction is to train your child to respond to your first command within 10 seconds—yes, 10 seconds! Now let's move on to review several specific learning theory principles that will help you better utilize the techniques in this book.

FOUR SOCIAL LEARNING PRINCIPLES

Studies show that parents who have some familiarity with social learning theory are better able to learn and master the techniques required to help oppositional children function more appropriately (Forehand and McMahon 1981). Below are four key social learning principles you should know to help you with your child management plan. They are based in part upon Forehand and McMahon's (1981) review of social learning theory.

1. *Most behavior is learned*—People generally learn behavioral patterns from others. To teach your child new behaviors, provide specific verbal prompts for desired behaviors and immediate verbal feedback. Model the specific behaviors you want your child to display and provide positive consequences for good behavior and negative consequences for bad behavior.

2. *Most behavior can be changed by the consequences of the behavior*—The consequences that parents provide either strengthen or weaken specific behaviors displayed by the child. To strengthen your child's appropriate behaviors, reward them. To weaken his inappropriate behaviors, ignore them or provide appropriate penalties.

3. *Positive reinforcement for good behavior preferably should be used more often than punishment for bad behavior*—Positive social reinforcers such as praise and enthusiastic attention are critical for helping children

learn appropriate behavioral and attitudinal skills. Praise good behavior immediately after the child has displayed good behavior. To help a child *learn* a new behavior, provide positive social reinforcement *every* time the child displays the desired behavior. Provide praise *intermittently* to help a child *maintain* a specific behavioral skill.

4. *Punishment for bad behavior preferably should be used sparingly*—Punishments such as "time out" help to eliminate oppositional, defiant, and aggressive behavior in children. For punishment to be effective it should be used as little as possible; occur immediately after the child displays the unwanted behavior; be carried out in the *same* manner each time it is used; be handled in a calm, businesslike way; and be of short duration.

This chapter has covered a variety of issues designed to prepare you for a meaningful change in approach to the specific problems of an oppositional, defiant, and aggressive child. Assuming that all systems are "go," let's now move on to part 2 of "Getting Ready for Change"— reviewing, and if necessary changing, your parenting philosophy.

2

What Is Your
Parenting Philosophy?

The parenting philosophy you adopt will either help or hinder your efforts to help your child. The goal of this chapter is to help you develop a rational parenting philosophy that will (1) increase the chances that you will be able to help your oppositional child function better; (2) improve the emotional atmosphere of your home; (3) give you several psychological tools to cope with your child's behavioral problems; and (4) prevent you from overreacting or underreacting to your child's defiance and aggression.

All human beings have beliefs about themselves, others, and the world. Some of the beliefs we hold are rational (helpful); some are irrational (unhelpful). Rational beliefs are ideas that can be supported by evidence; are flexible; fit with how the world works; generally, but not always, help you achieve your goals; and lead to moderate, appropriate displays of emotion and behavior (Ellis and Dryden 1987). Irrational beliefs are ideas that cannot be supported by evidence; are rigid and absolutistic; do not fit with how the world works; frequently prevent you from achieving your goals in life; and lead to disturbed, inappropriate displays of emotion and behavior (Ellis and Dryden 1987). As is the case for most parents, your approach to parenting is probably based on a combination of rational and irrational beliefs about your child and his defiant behavior. Use this chapter to self-diagnose any unhelpful beliefs you may have about your child and his disruptive behavior and to strengthen a rational parenting philosophy. Also, as you review this chapter, keep the following key point in mind: *your oppositional/defiant child does not make you enraged, depressed, or panicked.* You enrage, depress, or panic yourself based on the way you think about or evaluate your child's behavioral difficulties.

The rational parenting philosophy to strive for occupies the middle ground of four lines of thought commonly found in individuals and families. These lines of thought, originally discussed by Ellis (1975) and more recently by Huber and Baruth (1989), are (1) Issuing Demands♦Stating Preferences♦Not Caring; (2) Feeling Crushed♦Feeling Concern♦Seeing/Feeling Nothing; (3) Frustration Intolerance♦Frustration Tolerance♦Frustration Denial; (4) "Trashing" Others♦Acceptance of Others♦Worshiping Others. The beginning and the end of each of these lines of thought are extreme and irrational and will reduce your chances of helping your child learn new behaviors and attitudes (see Table 2–1). Read on and identify, tear up, and discard your areas of irrational thinking.

RATIONAL AND IRRATIONAL PARENTING ATTITUDES

1. *Issuing Demands♦Stating Preferences♦Not Caring*— Issuing demands, or "demandingness," is an attitude or

state of mind in which a parent, in Godlike fashion, thinks, "My children and others *must* behave in the way that I decree." This type of thinking is rigid, grandiose, and irrational, because there is no law of the universe that says that anyone, *even your children*, *must* or *should* behave in the way you demand. Demandingness does nothing more than set you up to be angry because, as you already know, your oppositional child *will* break your self-proclaimed laws. The psychological mechanism that leads to a "demanding" point of view is your tendency to transform your legitimate preferences and desires into rigid, intolerant, absolute demands. You tell yourself, "Because I *want* my child to show better behavior, he absolutely *must* do what I say." *This is not a logical conclusion* because, again, there is no law of the universe that says your child must, should, or ought to behave, though it would be highly preferable if he did.

TABLE 2–1. Rational and Irrational Parenting Attitudes

1. Issuing Demands	Stating Preferences	Not Caring
irrational	rational	irrational
2. Feeling Crushed	Feeling Concern	Seeing/Feeling Nothing
irrational	rational	irrational
3. Frustration Intolerance	Frustration Tolerance	Frustration Denial
irrational	rational	irrational
4. Trashing Others	Acceptance of Others	Worshiping Others
irrational	rational	irrational

Adapted from *Rational-Emotive Family Therapy: A Systems Perspective* by C. Huber and L. Baruth. New York: Springer 1989. Copyright © 1989 by Springer Publishing Co., Inc., New York 10012. Used by permission of the publisher.

At the other end of this line of thought is the attitude of not caring about your child and his oppositional behavior. Parents sometimes express this attitude by ignoring the child's troubles and dropping all expectations. At this point parental thinking is something like "My child is a hopeless case. I don't have the strength to care anymore. He can just do whatever he wants." The switch to not caring usually occurs after some intense, unsuccessful period of demandingness. In other words, when it becomes clear to parents that demandingness does not work, they will sometimes resort to washing their hands of the whole matter of trying to help an oppositional/defiant child learn new behavioral skills. Now let me ask: How is not caring going to help you achieve your goals for your child? Where is the *evidence* that not caring helps children function better?

The rational attitude to develop and *maintain* is one that consistently conveys your strong preference for your child to cooperate and obey your rules. Tell yourself, "I hope that my child will learn to cooperate, and I will stay involved as long as necessary to teach, guide, and influence him to do better, but he never *has* to." This type of thinking will reduce your anger and lead to more moderate feelings of concern and frustration when your child misbehaves.

2. *Feeling Crushed♦Feeling Concern♦Seeing/Feeling Nothing*—Feeling crushed or devastated is the state of mind in which a parent thinks: "It's horrible, terrible, and awful that my child is acting this way. I'm totally

crushed by his or her catastrophically bad behavior."
This type of thinking is irrational, because the words
horrible, terrible, and *awful* mean that something is 110
percent bad—worse than the worst thing that could ever
happen to a person (Ellis and Dryden 1987). Now, let
me ask: Is your child's bad behavior really horrible? Is
it even the worst thing that could ever happen to you,
like having your house burn down or having your whole
family die in a plane crash? To give up your "devastation" thinking, create a personal catastrophe scale that
will help you put your child's behavior problems in a
more realistic perspective. (See Table 2–2.) Also, stop
using the words *horrible, awful,* and *terrible.* Instead,
substitute the word *unfortunate.* It's *unfortunate* when
your oppositional child does not behave well, but hardly
a horrible catastrophe.

At the other end of this line of thinking is seeing/
feeling nothing (SFN). SFN, or *denial,* refers to a con-
scious or unconscious decision to block out or not
notice something that *does* exist. SFN expresses itself
through statements such as, "We have no problems in
our family," "Absolutely nothing is wrong with me or
my child," "We all feel fine," "Boys will be boys," and
so on. SFN (denial) and its close friend *minimization,*
the tendency to greatly downplay a problem, easily
allow parents to escape and *avoid* the hard work of helping an oppositional child. In the long run, however, a
denial state of mind will place your child at greater risk,
because you are not letting yourself see his problem or

TABLE 2–2. Personal Catastrophe Scale

10 = Horrible-Terrible-Awful = worse than the worst thing that could ever happen to me.
9 to 1 = Unfortunate events or circumstances.

Horrible	→	10 - Atom bomb destroys my state—everyone dies.
The worst	→	9 - My whole family dies.
		8 - Car accident leaves me paralyzed.
		7 - My spouse divorces me.
		6 - My house burns down.
		5 - I lose my job.
		4 - My child is oppositional and defiant.
		3 - My car is stolen.
		2 - I bounce a check.
		1 - I lose my comb.

possible solutions. In the meantime your child's bad behavioral habits are getting worse!

The rational ground between these extreme frames of reference is to acknowledge and admit that your defiant child has a problem and allow yourself to feel disappointment and concern rather than devastation or denial. Your disappointment and concern can be used to propel you toward creative solutions to your child's problems.

3. *Frustration Intolerance♦Frustration Tolerance♦ Frustration Denial*—Frustration *in*tolerance means that you often give up when things are hard. Frustration intolerance is expressed when a parent thinks: "I must get cooperation from my child easily and without ef-

fort, because I can't stand the physical and mental discomfort I feel when things are hard. My child should just know how to behave better on his own." This attitude leads to inconsistency in parenting because some parents irrationally believe that they should not have to work and sweat and "hang in there" to get results and, further, that working hard and tolerating discomfort would in some way be life threatening. It should be obvious that this type of thinking will prevent you from following through on this or any other plan to help your oppositional child. Effective parents frequently tolerate discomfort and frustration to create *consistency* in their approaches to problem solving with their children.

At the other extreme is frustration denial. Frustration denial is a defensive attitude used by some parents to ward off awareness of how much they actually fear or dread frustration and discomfort. Frustration denial is present when a parent thinks: "Because I don't want to notice how much I *can't stand* frustration and discomfort, I'll pretend that nothing bothers me. Yes, that's right, *nothing* bothers me." At best, this type of false self-reassurance produces superficial or half-hearted support for your child management plan because your underlying dread of discomfort is still present and influencing your behavior. To challenge your attempt not to notice your fear of discomfort, ask yourself: "Is it true that nothing bothers me? Do I really handle frustration and discomfort so well?" To challenge your core fear of discomfort, ask yourself: "Where is the evidence that I can't stand discomfort? Has frustration or discomfort ever killed anyone?" By shedding your frustration denial and tearing up your fear of discomfort, you will be better able to tolerate the very real discomfort and frustration you will at times experience in parenting an oppositional child.

The rational attitude to adopt is frustration *tolerance*. Genuine frustration tolerance will help you be consistent, prevent you from overreacting or giving up on your child, and allow you to withstand *with discomfort* displays of defiance, disobedience, and disrespect from your child. To develop frustration tolerance tell yourself: "Parenting an oppositional child is hard and frustrating but *not too hard*, and *I can handle it*. Without hard work and effort *every day* I will probably not achieve my goal of helping my child develop better behavioral habits. I really dislike it when my child is disobedient and disrespectful, but I'm not going to give up on my plan to help him."

4. *Trashing Others♦Acceptance of Others♦Worshiping Others*—Trashing others is the tendency to totally and globally put someone down or evaluate someone or your child as totally bad—100 percent bad. Trashing is based on the mistaken notion that you can judge another human being's worth *as a person* on the basis of his behavior. Trashing beliefs toward children usually takes the form: "Because you disobeyed me, you are a totally bad child who deserves to be severely pun-

ished." To avoid this extreme attitude, you need to challenge and throw out the unhelpful idea that a child's worth is determined by his or her behavior. It is appropriate to rate your child's behavior as good or bad, but his worth as a person is never in question. Also, for a person to be judged as totally bad he or she would have to behave badly 100 percent of the time, which is never the case, even for a criminal on death row!

It is equally irrational to increase the worth of another person or your child based on good behavior. This tendency is known as worshiping others, and it is expressed in thoughts like: "Because my child has done good deeds today and has restrained himself from acting badly, he is virtually a saint and really worthwhile as a person," or "My child's good behavior proves that he is a little angel, and his worth as a person is therefore elevated to near Godlike proportions." Worshiping others means you are still rating the worth of others on the basis of their behavior.

The rational alternative to these irrational extremes is to develop and maintain an attitude of *unconditional acceptance* of yourself as a parent and of your oppositional child. All human beings are equally worthwhile and all human beings, including your oppositional/ defiant child, are fallible. We sometimes succeed and sometimes fail, but our worth remains constant. Saints and criminals have the same value as human beings, though saints clearly behave better than criminals.

Summary

This chapter was designed to help you develop a philosophy of parenting that will increase the chances that you will be able to teach your child new behaviors. Overall, the optimal parental attitude toward the behaviorally troubled child is one in which parents (1) consistently communicate their strong desire for their child to do well; (2) use their frustration and disappointment to stimulate further problem solving; (3) tolerate uncomfortable feelings and sensations that go with parenting, particularly when setting limits for the child; and (4) communicate unconditional acceptance of the child. Several other attitudes will further increase the chances that your child will respond to the approach described in this book. Specifically, they are feelings of kindness toward the child, the capacity to provide limits and penalties in a firm yet loving way, and the capacity to *forgive* an oppositional child for being difficult.

COPING STATEMENTS FOR PARENTS OF OPPOSITIONAL CHILDREN

Practice the following coping statements *frequently* to support and sustain a rational parenting philosophy.

    1. *To promote a "preferring" or "desiring" state of mind*: (a) "I very much prefer and hope that my child

will learn to cooperate, but there is no law of the universe that says he ever has to." (b) "I am strong enough to remain in control while I communicate my preferences and expectations to my oppositional child." (c) "If I am getting overly angry, it means I am transforming my preferences into Godlike demands for good behavior from my child."

2. *To promote feelings of concern about the oppositional child's behavior:* (a) "It's unfortunate that my child is misbehaving, but hardly a catastrophe." (b) "Dealing with my child's oppositional and defiant behavior is not the worst thing that could happen to me." (c) "I can use my disappointment, frustration and concern about my child's misbehavior to help me search for solutions."

3. *To promote frustration tolerance:* (a) "Although I would like parenting to be easy, it mostly is not an easy job." (b) "I will not get results from my chosen child management plan unless I persist through the hard times and tolerate many uncomfortable feelings." (c) "I *can* stand it when I feel uncomfortable or when I have to exert myself to make my plan for my child work." (d) "Though I do not like it, I *can* handle it when my child is disobedient or disrespectful."

4. *To promote acceptance of the oppositional/defiant child:* (a) "My oppositional child is always a worthwhile person though I may not like his behavior." (b) "All human beings, including children, are fallible. We

sometimes do things well, but often make mistakes." (c) "I can forgive my oppositional child for being difficult." (d) "Even if my child never gets better I can still choose to accept him and find things in our relationship to enjoy."

3

Winning Cooperation from Your Child

A nonviolent, praise-oriented home environment motivates the oppositional/defiant child to display better attitudes and behaviors. The goal of this chapter is to provide you with a range of easy-to-use techniques to promote cooperative, prosocial, nonviolent behavior in your child. The techniques in this chapter are described under three headings: (1) shaping the tone of the home environment, (2) positive social reinforcement, and (3) privileges and rewards.

SHAPING THE EMOTIONAL AND BEHAVIORAL TONE OF THE HOME ENVIRONMENT

Remember, as the parent you are responsible for establishing and maintaining the emotional and behavioral tone of your home. Some homes have an overall tone of anger, hostility, and unending, unresolvable conflict. Other homes have a sad, unhappy, depressive atmosphere. Still others have an overly fearful, anxious tone and a pervasive sense that the outside world is unsafe. In homes such as these, angry, unhappy, or fearful parents may not be able to fully respond to the child's emotional need for security or to fully and wholeheartedly work with a behaviorally troubled child to help him recover from his behavioral problem. Also, children may themselves become so angry, unhappy, or fearful that they are not able to learn new behaviors and attitudes.

The optimal home atmosphere to strive for is non-violent, relatively structured, upbeat or positive, praise oriented, and rich in incentives for good behavior. In shaping the tone of your home you want to communicate to your children that you and your spouse are in charge of the home and that you are serious about children following rules and directions. It is also important to be clear about your rules and expectations. Below are eight guidelines you can use to create a more positive atmosphere in your home.

1. *Be a role model.* I discussed this in Chapter 1, but it is so important it is worth mentioning again. It is critical that you model the behaviors and attitudes you want your child to learn. As much as you can, demonstrate cooperation, kindness, impulse control, frustration tolerance, patience, playfulness, and nonaggressive ways to solve problems. This will greatly contribute to a more positive home atmosphere and will set a powerful example for your child to follow.

2. *Post the rules of the home.* The simple technique of posting your expectations and rules eliminates the possibility that your oppositional child may not know what your rules and expectations are. By writing down daily chores and tasks and posting them, you also reduce your child's sense that you are an arbitrary "dic-

tator" who sometimes makes pronouncements about the rules and at other times ignores the rules.

3. *Phrase directions as statements, not questions.* It is common for parents to tell children to do tasks with questions. For example, many parents would say "James, would you go clean your bedroom now?" James's response might well be: "Well, now that you mention it, *no!*" Telling your child to do a chore with a question implies he has a choice, when in fact you have no intention of making certain tasks optional. Deliver your directions to your child in command form with a businesslike tone of voice. Reduce all other distractions such as television, and establish eye contact when you are giving directions to your child. If necessary, have your child repeat your directions. Using good "direction technique" conveys to the child that you are serious about what you want him to do. Knowing that parents mean business helps oppositional children to become more cooperative.

4. *Resolve conflicts privately with your spouse or partner.* It is generally advisable to work out your child management disagreements privately with your spouse or partner. In this way you and your spouse/partner can present yourselves to the children as a unified co-parenting team. Open and heated parental disagreements often result in the child's seeing one parent as "the bad guy" and the other as "the good guy." This type of split is not helpful for either the parents or the child.

Except in abusive situations, you should publicly support your spouse or partner's judgment when he or she is in conflict with your child, even if you privately disagree. If you do disagree with what your spouse is doing at a given point, talk it over with him or her later when the problem is behind you. Then work out a plan for handling the problem differently the next time it occurs.

5. *Eliminate all television shows and video games that display violent acts.* We now know that children who are prone to acting aggressively can be stimulated to display aggression following exposure to brutal scenes on television. Watching violence and aggression on television probably leads oppositional, defiant, aggressive children to imitate what they have seen on television, to believe the world is a violence-ridden place, and to believe they are justified in acting violently because they see others acting that way on television (King and Noshpitz 1991).

Unfortunately, many of the television shows currently produced for consumption by children are filled with acts of violence and brutality. At present some of the most popular children's shows are Mighty Morphin Power Rangers, Biker Mice from Mars, Skysurfer Strike Force, Mega Man, V. R. Troopers, SWAT Kats: The Radical Squadron, Road Runner cartoons, Street Sharks, Fantastic Four, Exosquad, Teknoman, and Superhuman Samurai Syber-Squad. Characters in these shows largely have no impulse control, no frustration tolerance, and no ability to solve problems nonviolently. Across the board these characters slam, crush, blast, flatten, shatter, and explode each other time and time again. Viewing such scenes for hours on end may deepen a violent or aggressive problem-solving "groove" in your child's mind. It may also make your child insensitive to the rights and feelings of other people.

For all of these reasons I recommend that you eliminate *all* such shows from your child's daily television diet. Part of the remedy for childhood aggression is *elimination of aggressive models, massive exposure to nonviolent models,* and a clear signal from parents that nonviolent methods of problem solving are valued. If your child protests your decision to eliminate violent TV shows, tell him that until he consistently shows more concern, kindness, and respect for others, all such television shows will be banned.

6. *Actively introduce your child to books and videos that contain themes of kindness, cooperation, sharing, and caring about others.* Frequent exposure to nonviolent, *prosocial* models of human interaction may further help your child develop the necessary inner resources to display kindness, cooperation, and concern for others more frequently (Strayhorn 1988). Try to find some time each day to enjoy a prosocial story or video with your child. Your local librarian or bookstore/videostore owner or your child's teacher can help you search for appropriate stories to share with your child.

7. *Show respect and concern for your child's other parent.* Under all circumstances show respect and con-

cern for your child's other parent. Criticizing, blaming, or insulting your child's other parent in your child's presence is like criticizing, blaming, or insulting *half* of your child (Porter-Thal 1994). By showing respect to your child's other parent you will improve the atmosphere of your home, model tolerance and self-control for your child, and keep your child from being caught in the middle of parental crossfire.

When parents have divorced or separated, one or both individuals may become so bitter and angry that they vow to make life as miserable as possible for each other. A parent who remains angry and unforgiving toward a former spouse sets a poor example for children on how to deal with difficult life situations. Children are also often embarrassed and scared by their divorced parents' immature, playground-like squabbles and hostile exchanges of criticism. No matter how wronged you feel by your former spouse or partner, try to bury the hatchet. If you consistently show respect to your child's other parent, your child will love you for showing maturity and self-control. If your child's other parent continues to try to make your life miserable, don't go back down to that level. Over time your child will know which parent is in control and which parent has a problem.

8. *Do not bring up yesterday's problems.* Yesterday is history. You can do nothing to change what has already happened, so why bring it up? Dredging up past problems only makes others, including children, resent-

ful. Make each day a new opportunity for things to be better, and keep your sights on the future.

Summary

In setting the tone of your home, you and your spouse/partner need to let your oppositional child know that (1) you (the parents) are in charge; (2) you expect your posted directions and rules to be followed; (3) you will model the behaviors you want your child to display; (4) you and your spouse support and trust each other's judgment regarding child management strategies; (5) you respect your child's other parent; (6) nonviolent ways of solving problems are valued; and (7) your sights are focused on the future. Now that you have worked on these issues, let's move on to positive social reinforcement.

POSITIVE SOCIAL REINFORCEMENT

Positive social reinforcement means that you pay enthusiastic attention to what your child is doing well or to any small steps your child takes toward a more cooperative attitude and more appropriate behaviors. All of the techniques in this section are forms of positive social reinforcement. To really help an oppositional/defiant child function better, you should plan to use all of the following techniques simultaneously unless otherwise specified.

Positive social reinforcement (praise) for specific prosocial behaviors—for example, cooperation, kindness, sharing, honesty—trains your child to display such behaviors more frequently. Since you have an endless supply of praise, you should be very generous in dispensing it to your child. Over time your child will internalize your "praising voice" and begin to praise himself for displaying appropriate, cooperative behavior. For your praise to be most effective it should be aimed at specific behaviors and attitudes, delivered immediately, and communicated with enthusiasm. When you praise your child, the tone of your voice is especially important. Be sure it has a clear, upward swing that communicates *genuine* pleasure and delight over your child's good behavior. The enthusiasm in your voice is a "melody" that children love to hear. Your praise will also be strengthened when combined with nonverbal signs of approval—a smile, a wink, a thumbs-up sign—and physical displays of warmth and approval, such as a hug, a pat on the back, or a gentle tousling of the hair.

Below are five ways in which you can give positive social reinforcement to your child each day. Provide such positive reinforcement in doses two to three times greater than the amount of punishment you deliver each day.

1. *Pay attention to your child's good behavior—* Over the course of a day increase your ability to notice what your child is doing well. If you believe you cannot find anything positive in your oppositional child's behavior you need to scan more closely for appropriate behavior. Research shows that children who are oppositional and defiant do not act this way all the time (Barkley 1987). Even the most difficult children display some good behavior each day.

Examples:

"Jason, you're doing a very nice job of using your imagination and playing quietly right now."

"James, thank you for putting your dinner plate in the sink. That was helpful."

"Sara, I'm pleased that you started to brush your teeth as soon as I told you to. I like it when you follow directions. Good girl!"

"Susan, I really like how nicely you've been playing with your brother for the past few minutes."

2. *Command–compliance training periods—* This is a simple technique described by Barkley (1987). The technique stems from the idea that the oppositional/ defiant child is relatively weak in the skill of being compliant or cooperative. Thus the child needs lots of "cooperation practice" to strengthen the skill of being cooperative. You can do command–compliance training periods with your child once or twice a day; they're very easy to do. (You do not need to tell your child he

is involved in a command–compliance training period.) The training technique is as follows: At some point during the day call your child over to you and over the course of 5 minutes give him two to four simple directions that require *no effort*. For example, when you are cooking dinner call your child into the kitchen and give several directions, such as "Please hand me the salad dressing," "Get me a spoon," "Hand me the potholder." Each time your child responds to your command provide praise. If your child does not respond, wait a minute and then try a different simple command. If your child still does not respond, abandon the command–compliance training attempt and try again later. Again, command–compliance training provides your child with extra cooperation practice and exposes him to the social benefits of being cooperative, that is, he receives praise. This technique should be used for two to four weeks or until your child begins to display better cooperation skills.

Examples:

Dad is working on the car in the driveway. Tommy is playing in the front yard.

DAD: "Tommy, come here for a minute."

TOMMY: "What, Dad?"

DAD: "Hand me that yellow screwdriver."

Tommy goes to the toolbox, gets the screwdriver, and brings it to his father.

TOMMY: "Here, Dad."

DAD: "Thanks for your help, Tommy. I appreciate it when you follow directions."

Dad then creates two or three more simple tasks for Tommy to do, each time providing praise.

Mom is reading a book in the living room. Katie is coloring pictures in her bedroom.

MOM: "Katie, come here please."

KATIE: "What is it, Mom? I was coloring."

MOM: "I know, but I'd like you to get me the bowl of potato chips from the dining room table."

Katie goes to the dining room, gets the bowl of chips, and brings it to her mother.

MOM: "Thanks, sweetie. I appreciate it when you follow directions. Would you like a potato chip?"

KATIE: "Okay."

MOM: "Katie, before you go back to coloring, please hand me that magazine on the table."

Katie goes to the table, gets the magazine, and hands it to Mom.

MOM: "Thanks, Katie. I appreciate your help."

3. *The nightly review*—This is a wonderful technique developed by Strayhorn (1988). The technique involves spending a few minutes each evening reviewing with your child some of the positive things he has done that day. Specifically, the nightly review is a time for parents to celebrate with the child some progress he has made that day in the areas of being cooperative,

honest, patient, helpful, or kind to others. The review can be done at dinnertime, shortly before bedtime, or when you're tucking your child in for the night. The nightly review is a helpful way to deliver some additional positive reinforcement to your child.

Examples:

Dad is tucking Sarah in for the night.

DAD: "Sarah, I was just remembering how you held the front door open for me this afternoon when I was bringing the groceries in from the car. That was very kind of you and helpful. This morning I also noticed that you shared some of your toys with your brother. I'm very proud of you for sharing."

Shortly before bedtime Mom talks to Kyle.

MOM: "Kyle, you were really a good sport today when we had to cancel our trip to the park. You stayed calm and were able to find some other ways of having fun. Also, I really liked it when you told the truth about taking that quarter from your brother. Good job."

4. *Proudly discuss your child's progress with your spouse or partner*—This technique is an indirect way of providing positive social reinforcement to your child. Each day take a few minutes to proudly discuss with your spouse or partner the progress your child has made that day. If you are a single parent, you may, as an alternative, get on the telephone and call Aunt Millie or a friend to convey your pleasure in your child's progress.

Just be sure your child is within earshot when you use this technique. Children love to feel that their parents are boasting or bragging about them.

Examples:

Mom and Dad are talking in the living room and Jeff walks by.

MOM: "Come here, Jeff, let me give you a hug."

Jeff goes to his mother and sits next to her on the sofa.

MOM turns to DAD: "Jim, guess what Jeff did today? He got dressed this morning quickly without a fuss. This afternoon he fed the dog as soon as I asked him to. He's doing a great job of following directions today."

DAD says to MOM: "Our boy is really trying hard to be more cooperative. That's terrific!"

Dad and Susan are bringing groceries in from the market. Mom greets them at the front door.

DAD says to MOM: "Laura, Susan was a real help at the store. She stayed close to me and didn't beg for treats. She also helped me push the shopping cart. I really enjoyed her company and her help."

MOM replies: "I've also noticed that Susan is trying to be more helpful. This morning she helped me take out the trash. I'm really proud of her for showing such a cooperative attitude today."

5. *Spend 20 minutes per day with your child in a "special time" activity*—This technique described by Barkley (1987) is very important. It stems from the idea

that by paying attention to your child's good play behavior you will stir in your child a stronger desire to follow your rules and directions. In other words, it will help your child *want* to be more cooperative.

Initiate the special time activity by telling your child you would like to spend some time with him doing something fun. Let your child pick the activity, and then simply enjoy the activity with your child. While playing with your child be sure to praise his or her good play behavior. For example, if your child picked a coloring activity, you might comment on how well he is staying inside the borders of the figures on the page or what nice colors he has chosen to use. Whatever the activity is—arts and crafts, board games, fantasy play—comment frequently on your child's playfulness and good ideas during the play. If your child becomes disruptive or is not able to play by the rules, tell him that special time is over and that you and he will play again tomorrow. Provide seven "special times" for your child during the first week (one 20-minute special time per day) and five special times per week thereafter indefinitely.

To appreciate the power of this technique, take a moment to think about the best boss you ever worked for. He or she probably was a person who had a good sense of humor, paid attention to your work, was supportive, helpful, and attentive. I'd bet money that boss stirred in you a desire to work hard and do a good job. The special time technique helps you treat your child like the *best boss* you ever had!

Examples:
Mom and Kyle are playing checkers.
Mom: "Kyle, you really are thinking of some clever moves today. That's great."

Dad and Lisa are playing tag on the front lawn.
Dad: "Lisa, you're such a fast runner I can hardly ever catch you. I'm impressed."

Dad and Daniel are looking at the pictures in a nature book.
Dad: "Dan, I really like it that you like to learn about animals and insects. You're a smart guy with a good mind."

Mom and Susan are out on a walk and Susan has been pointing out squirrels and birds.
Mom: "Susan, you really are good at spotting all the little creatures in our neighborhood. Let's see if we can spot some more."

PRIVILEGES AND REWARDS

Privileges should always be used as incentives to help an oppositional child display greater cooperation toward daily chores and self-care responsibilities. The technique is simple and contains the following two steps: (1) define all of the activities your child enjoys each day as privileges—having a friend over, watching television, listening to music, bike riding, playing baseball, playing in the yard, or going to a friend's home; (2) allow use of these privileges only after your child has completed necessary chores and/or self-care tasks. The basic message to your child is "You work before you play." Oppositional children usually begin to take daily responsibilities more seriously once it is clear that privileges are contingent upon satisfactory completion of work.

Material rewards can be used sparingly as incentives for cooperative behavior. Material rewards are inexpensive items such as baseball cards, stickers, candy treats, tiny toys, and comic books. Use material rewards in relation to specific chores or self-care responsibilities that your child finds *especially difficult* to accomplish. The prospect of some immediately available tangible reward usually helps to encourage cooperation from an oppositional child. As your child begins to display competence in a previously difficult area, provide lots of positive social reinforcement, that is, praise and enthusiastic attention, and gradually phase out the material rewards. For example, a child whose morning dressing routine has improved substantially in response to positive reinforcement, and a small "grab bag" toy each day, could be told that his toy would now be available on Fridays provided he gets dressed each school day without a hassle. After several weeks the tangible rewards can be stopped altogether and the new areas of competence maintained by positive social reinforcement alone.

Parents are sometimes reluctant to offer material rewards for cooperative behavior on the grounds that such an approach is a form of bribery, which it is not. Remember, bribery occurs when one person tries to entice another person to do something unethical or illegal. There is nothing unethical or illegal about trying to help an oppositional/defiant child learn better social, behavioral, and attitudinal skills. The incentives and rewards you offer to your child in exchange for his cooperative behavior are no different than the paychecks you receive from your employer for the hard work you give at the office.

As you prepare to use privileges and rewards to promote cooperation from your child, keep the following additional tips in mind: (1) tell your child the specific tasks and chores you expect him to start and complete each day; (2) explain the specific privileges and rewards he will gain through cooperative behavior and write them down on a chore/reward menu; (3) if your child does not earn a privilege or reward, he still has to complete the chore/task he was told to do before he is allowed to do anything else. Once the chore/task has been completed, he can engage in play activities other than the ones listed on the chore/reward menu; and (4) if your child fails to earn a reward or privilege and he accuses you of taking away his privileges, calmly tell him that *he took his privileges away from himself* by *choosing* not to complete a specific task or set of tasks.

It is usually advisable to break the day into morning, afternoon, and evening routines. Start each segment of the day with a positive attitude. Communicate to your child that each part of the day is a new opportunity to display chore and task competence and cooperative attitudes and behaviors. Below is an example of how a typical chore/reward program might look for an 8-year-old oppositional child named Richard.

1. *Richard's morning routine*—Get up and make bed, wash up, get dressed, brush teeth, comb hair, get book bag ready. If Richard completes all of these tasks without a hassle by 7:30 A.M., he earns a reward before he goes to school. If a hassle occurs or tasks are not completed on time, no rewards are provided.

Possible morning rewards—Eat breakfast in front of the television while watching a nonviolent show, wear some "cool" sneakers or clothes to school, earn 50 cents allowance, get a special snack treat in lunch bag, receive a small toy out of a grab bag, read a nonviolent comic book for a few minutes.

2. *Richard's afternoon routine*—Change into playclothes, do homework, empty the trash. If Richard completes all of these tasks by 3:45 P.M., he gets his privileges as a reward. If tasks are not done on time or if there is a hassle, rewards and privileges are not available.

Possible afternoon rewards (one or several may be used)—Play outside, have a friend over, watch half an hour of nonviolent television, ride bike, play with nonviolent video games, go to a friend's house, go for a walk with mom, do an arts and crafts activity.

3. *Richard's evening routine*—Help clean up after dinner, feed dog, take bath, brush teeth, get into pajamas. If Richard completes all of these tasks by 7 P.M., he earns privileges and rewards. If tasks are not completed by 7 P.M., rewards are not given.

Possible evening rewards—15 minutes of wrestling with dad, special snack, half an hour of nonviolent television, bedtime 15 minutes later, extra bedtime story, play a card game with Mom.

Summary

For the sake of review, keep the following points in mind to promote cooperative behavior in your child: (1) work to establish a nonviolent, praise-oriented home environment; (2) be a role model; (3) post the rules of the home; (4) phrase directions as statements, not questions; (5) resolve conflicts privately with your spouse or partner; (6) eliminate all television shows, cartoons, and video games that display violent acts; (7) actively introduce your child to stories and videos with kindness themes; (8) show respect and concern for your child's other parent; (9) do not bring up yesterday's problems; (10)

frequently "catch" your child at being good; (11) use command–compliance training periods for two to four weeks in the early stages of work with your child; (12) provide additional positive social reinforcement to your child in the form of the nightly review; (13) proudly discuss your child's progress with your spouse or partner each day; (14) spend 20 minutes per day with your child in a special activity; (15) use privileges and rewards as incentives to promote cooperative behavior.

The consistent use of these positive methods of influence should, over time, produce more cooperative behaviors and attitudes in your child. Some children, however, also require penalties to help them learn more appropriate behaviors. So let's move on to talk about penalties for noncompliance, defiance, and aggression.

4

Penalties for Noncompliance, Defiance, and Aggression

The skillful use of penalties for noncompliance, defiance, and aggression can significantly reduce such behaviors in the behaviorally troubled child. In this chapter you will learn (1) how to deliver penalties effectively; (2) several specific penalty techniques, including the ignoring and time-out procedures; and (3) what to do if your child refuses to go to time-out or is unable to calm down while on time-out.

Remember, noncompliant, defiant, and aggressive behavior in children may be learned behaviors, that is, some of your child's disruptive, noncompliant behaviors can be thought of as learned "bad habits." The good news is that learned bad behaviors can be suppressed or buried beneath newly learned good behaviors. A child management approach that consistently uses positive social reinforcement for appropriate behavior and penalties for inappropriate behavior stands a reasonable chance of helping the oppositional child acquire better behavioral habits.

PENALTY SKILLS GROUND RULES

To get started, there are several penalty ground rules you need to keep in mind to increase the chances that your penalties will be effective. Carefully review each of the following guidelines.

1. Do not try to use words, reason, or logic when providing your child with a penalty. Trying to reason with your child in the midst of a conflict is like saying to him or her, "Before you agree to accept your penalty, please let me convince you of how right I am that you need a penalty."

2. Do not display emotion when providing penalties. As much as possible try to remain calm and businesslike when implementing a penalty. If you become overly emotional, it will reinforce (reward) your child's disruptive/oppositional behavior and may even lead him to believe he is in some kind of exciting game with you.

3. Tolerate the frustration and discomfort you will likely experience when you see your child upset over his penalty. Some parents irrationally believe that children must never be frustrated or upset. Thus, when the child begins to display distress, parents back off from following through on a penalty. Remember, both you and your child *will survive* the distress each of you experiences when a penalty technique is used.

4. Do not start to use any of the following penalty techniques if you believe that an emotional reaction such as guilt or anxiety may prevent you from following through with a penalty. If the thought of setting limits or delivering penalties to your child stirs emotions that could possibly interfere with your ability to set limits,

tell yourself that "setting limits and following through on penalties is a form of love. My child will be relieved that I am setting limits." If you still feel reluctant to set limits for your child, consult a therapist to remove your emotional blocks to limit setting and the use of penalties. Then begin to use the penalty techniques in this chapter.

5. Before using the time-out procedure, select a very dull, boring place in your home to use as the time-out spot. Good places to use are hallways, laundry rooms, and corners. Whatever place you choose should be safe and free of any objects your child could use as toys or distractions while on time-out.

6. Remember, deliver penalties immediately, in a businesslike tone of voice, and in the *same way* every time. Also, use penalties consistently outside the home. All of the following penalty techniques can be used in public—restaurants, church, stores, or when visiting the home of a friend.

7. Before you start to use the penalties described in this chapter, tell your child about the penalty plan. Describe how you will use the ignoring and time-out procedures and what will happen if he refuses to go to time-out. Then implement the penalties.

I recommend three specific penalty techniques to decrease oppositional, defiant, and aggressive behavior in children. The techniques may appear simple, but skill is required to use them effectively. The techniques are ignoring, time-out, and loss of privileges.

THE IGNORING TECHNIQUE

Ignoring is a powerful way to decrease misbehavior and is somewhat easier to use than time-out. When using the ignoring technique keep in mind the social learning principle that *behavior that does not receive attention tends to weaken or disappear.* Ignoring can be used for many low-level inappropriate behaviors such as whining, hounding, not taking no for an answer, yelling, swearing, and temper tantrums. Do not use the ignoring technique for any behavior that is potentially dangerous or when your child may be about to harm someone or destroy property. The ignoring technique should be used as long as the child is engaging in the inappropriate behavior you are trying to eliminate (Forehand and McMahon 1981).

Keep in mind that when you first begin to use the ignoring technique, you may see an increase in the disruptive or inappropriate behaviors you are ignoring. This increase is commonly known as an "extinction burst" (Kazdin 1994). It reflects your child's effort to coerce you into paying attention to his inappropriate behavior. Tough it out through this phase; usually the behavior you are ignoring will diminish after some period of time.

The ignoring technique has three components described by Forehand and McMahon (1981): (1) *No eye contact or non-verbal cues.* Do not look at or gesture to your child. (2) *No verbal contact.* Do not say anything, especially if your child demands to know why he is being ignored. (3) *No physical contact.* Do not respond if your child tries to tug on you, hug you, or sit on your lap. If necessary, leave the room to stop your child from initiating physical contact. Once your child has stopped the inappropriate behavior you are ignoring, be sure to return quickly to the use of positive social reinforcement for good behavior.

THE TIME-OUT PROCEDURE

Time-out is really an extreme form of ignoring, used when the child's behavior is so unacceptable that removal from the social group is necessary. Time-out communicates a powerful message to the child. The message is: "Your behavior is now so unacceptable you need to be isolated to rethink and readjust your behavior." Time-out can be used to help a child improve at following directions, following through on chores, and developing better self-help skills. It can also be used to reduce testing, manipulation, defiance, and aggression.

The following general guidelines apply to all of the time-out procedures described below. (1) Time-out should be limited to 5 minutes. (2) Time-out does not begin until your child settles down. Do not start the 5-minute time-out if your child is screaming and yelling. If he is upset, tell him that his time-out will begin when he is relatively calm. (3) Release from time-out is always a "contingent release"; before your child is released from time-out he must agree to do the task he was told to do in the first place or to apologize for an act of aggression, property destruction, or disruptive behavior.

1. *Time-out for not following directions*—The time-out procedure for use with a child who is not following directions is as follows: Give your child a clear command ("Jimmy, put your dirty clothes in the hamper") and wait 5 seconds. If your child follows your direction, provide enthusiastic attention or praise immediately. If your child does not follow your direction, issue a warning ("Jimmy, if you do not put your clothes in the hamper now you *will* receive a time-out"). Wait 5 more seconds. If your child does the desired task, provide enthusiastic attention or praise. If your child does not respond, send your child immediately to time-out ("Okay, Jimmy, you did not put your clothes in the hamper. Go to time-out now"). Figure 4–1 illustrates this time-out procedure.

2. *Time-out for manipulation, hounding, badgering, interrupting, disrespectful talk, and not taking no for an answer*—Ignoring is often the best way to approach hounding, badgering, disrespectful talk, and not taking no for an answer. For some oppositional children, however, the use of time-out extinguishes such behaviors better than the ignoring technique.

The time-out technique for these unwanted behaviors is as follows: Your child displays one of the above-mentioned behaviors. Tell your child to stop the unde-

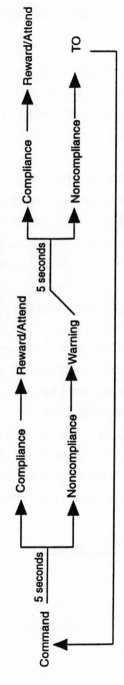

Figure 4-1. The Parental Command–Consequence Procedure

From *Helping the Noncompliant Child* (p. 78) by R.L. Forehand and R.J. McMahon. New York: Guilford 1981. Copyright © 1981 by Guilford Publications, Inc. Used by permission of the publisher.

sirable behavior he is displaying ("Steven, stop hounding me right now") and wait 5 seconds. If your child
stops the inappropriate behavior, praise him for showing self-control. If he persists with the undesirable
behavior, issue a warning ("Steven, if you do not stop
hounding me right now you will receive a time-out")
and wait 5 seconds. If your child stops hounding, you
provide praise for showing self-control. If your child
persists with the undesirable behavior, send him to
time-out. ("Okay, you did not stop hounding me. Go to
time-out now.") Figure 4–1 also illustrates this form
of time-out.

3. *Time-out for physical aggression or property
destruction*—The time-out procedure can also be used
when your child engages in physical aggression or property destruction. In these situations no warning is necessary. Simply tell him that for hitting or breaking property he will have a 5-minute time-out. Again, time-out
does not begin until he has settled down. Also, release
from time-out is contingent upon your child's apologiz-
ing for the act of aggression or property destruction and
promising not to engage in that behavior again.

What to Do If Your Child Refuses
to Go to Time-out

Parents often wonder what to do if the child refuses to
go to time-out. If your child has received a time-out and

defiantly refuses to go, use the following technique described by Kavanagh and colleagues (1991). To the original 5 minutes add one extra minute of time-out for each refusal to go to time-out, up to a maximum of 10 minutes. If your child still refuses to go after receiving 10 minutes of time-out, tell him he now has a choice —either go to time-out for 10 minutes or immediately lose an important privilege such as playing outside for 2 hours or losing television for 2 hours. If your child still refuses to go to time-out, remove the privilege and move on.

What to Do If Your Child Will Not Calm Down While on Time-out

When sent to time-out, some oppositional children refuse or are unable to calm themselves and persist in displaying loud, disruptive, defiant behavior. If your child refuses to settle down after 15 minutes and serve his minimum sentence of 5 minutes, release him from the time-out attempt and instead remove a privilege for 2 hours (Kavanagh et al. 1991). When you do this, be sure to explain why you are changing the penalty: "John, since you are unable to accept a time-out now, you will instead not be able to ride your bike for the next 2 hours." Over time your child will probably learn that it is easier to take a 5-minute time-out than endure a 2-hour privilege loss.

SOME ADDITIONAL PENALTY TIPS

1. Once you tell your child to go to time-out, *that's it!* No second chances. Some children will try to manipulate their way out of time-out by scrambling to do the task they were told to do or by stopping an undesirable behavior and promising to be good. If this happens, tell your child, "Too late. Go to time-out now. You will do what you were told when time-out is over."

2. Ignore any defiant talk that your child may direct at you while he heads for the time-out spot.

3. Ignore your child if he tells you or acts as if he could care less about your penalties. Believe me, your child cares.

4. If your child reacts angrily, defiantly, or aggressively to the news that he has received a time-out, do *not* get into a punishment spiral of adding more and more punishments to the original 5 minutes of time-out. Remain calm and use your penalty skills to enforce the original time-out or, alternatively, remove a privilege.

5. If your child messes something on the way to time-out, he should clean up the mess after time-out and then do the task he was originally told to do.

Now that you have learned a variety of ways to deliver positive social reinforcement and penalties, it is time to aim these methods of influence at your child in a way that helps to strengthen specific social, behavioral, and attitudinal skills. Let's move on. You're doing great!

5

Building Social
and Behavioral Skills

By harnessing the combined powers of positive social reinforcement, penalties, role modeling, and other methods of influence, you can help your child learn specific social and behavioral skills. In this chapter, which is based upon the work of Joseph Strayhorn (1988), you will learn to identify specific social and behavioral goals for your child and to develop a "high priority skills" workplan to promote social, behavioral, and attitudinal competence in your child.

IDENTIFYING BEHAVIORAL GOALS

To identify social and behavioral goals for your child, you first need to review his or her main behavioral problems, or "symptoms," such as physical aggression, lying, and oppositional behavior. Inappropriate problem behaviors like these can be viewed as indicators of specific skill weaknesses in your child (Strayhorn 1988). For example, a child who is aggressive toward others is relatively weak in the skill of being kind and gentle to others. Lying reflects relative weakness in the skill of giving accurate and truthful answers. An oppositional/ defiant attitude reflects some weakness in the skill of following directions and maintaining a cooperative/ respectful attitude, and so forth.

As your child becomes more competent in the specific skill areas that you will identify as his high priority "skill goals," his main behavioral problems should fade significantly. Table 5–1 lists some of the problem behaviors that oppositional children typically display. Next to each problem behavior is the desired social or behavioral skill required to reduce the symptomatic behavior. Select three or four of the skills you *most* want your child to display right away and use them as the first set of high priority skill-goals for your child to work on. As your child begins to display competence in one or several of the initial skill areas, you can add new goals to the workplan. If your child has a particular problem that is not identified in Table 5–1, a consultation with a behaviorally oriented therapist might help you develop other specific prosocial goals for your child.

THE HIGH PRIORITY SKILLS WORKPLAN

After selecting your child's goals, you can write a high priority skills workplan using a form like the one displayed in Table 5–2. This format allows you to record your child's main symptoms, list his high-priority skill goals, identify the specific methods of influence you will use to help your child achieve these goals, and remain focused on all aspects of the plan. The instructions for completing the workplan are as follows.

Table 5–1. Symptoms/Skills Menu

Symptoms	Skills/Goals
1. Oppositional attitude	1. Cooperative attitude
2. Defiant talk/verbal abuse	2. Respectful talk
3. Aggression toward others	3. Kind and gentle with others
4. Lying	4. Accurate and truthful answers
5. Stealing/property destruction	5. Respect for others' property
6. "Poor sport" when frustrated (low frustration tolerance), includes tantruming, arguing, badgering	6. "Good sport" when frustrated (high frustration tolerance), good-natured acceptance of not getting own way
7. Acting before thinking (impulsivity)	7. Thinking before acting (impulse control)
8. Swearing	8. Clean talk
9. Cheating	9. Playing fair
10. Not sharing	10. Sharing with others
11. Blaming others	11. Admitting mistakes
12. Not talking about ideas and feelings	12. Talking about ideas and feelings
13. Teasing peers	13. Talking nicely to peers
14. Screaming/making loud noises	14. Talking in a normal tone of voice
15. Not following directions	15. Following directions

1. *The problem areas lines*—On these lines note the three or four main symptoms you see as major problem areas for your child. Remember, these symptoms reflect specific skill weaknesses in your child.

2. *The skills/goals column*—In the skills/goals column list the three or four high-priority skills you want

Table 5-2. High-Priority Skills Work Plan

Child's Name ___Kyle___   Age ___8___   Date of this Plan ___5/19/96___

Problem Areas   1) Physical aggression toward others   2) Poor sport when frustrated

               3) Noncompliant and oppositional re: chores & tasks   4) Defiant talk

PARENTAL METHODS OF INFLUENCE

Skills (Goals for Child)	Consequences	Modeling	Practice	Others Methods of Influence
1. Kind & gentle with others →	Enthusiastic attention	Parents model kindness and concern for others	All Family Interaction	1) Nightly review 2) Proudly discuss child's progress 3) No violent TV or cartoons 4) Stories & videos with kindness themes
(Physical aggression →)	Automatic time-out			
2. Good sport when frustrated →	Enthusiastic attention	Parents model being good sports when frustrated	All Family Interaction	1) Nightly review 2) Proudly discuss child's progress
(Poor sport →)	Ignore			

3. Follow directions → Cooperative attitude (Noncompliant →)	Enthusiastic attention Command-Warning Time-out	Parents model cooperative attitudes	All Family Interaction	1) Nightly review 2) Proudly discuss child's progress 3) Command–compliance training 4) 20 min. special time each day
4. Respectful talk → (Defiant talk →)	Enthusiastic attention Ignore	Parents model respectful talk	All Family Interaction	1) Nightly review 2) Proudly discuss child's progress

Adapted from *The Competent Child: An Approach to Psychotherapy and Preventive Mental Health* by J.M. Strayhorn. New York: Guilford 1988. Copyright © 1988 by Guilford Publications, Inc. Used by permission of the publisher.

your child to learn. In the parentheses under each high priority skill list the related symptom again. I'll tell you why in the next paragraph.

3. *The consequences column*—In this column list the positive consequences you will provide your child when he displays the desired high-priority skill (e.g., praise or enthusiastic attention). At the bottom of the box, next to the line in parentheses, list the negative consequences you will use when the unwanted symptom or problem emerges (e.g. ignoring or time-out).

4. *The modeling column*—In the modeling column make a note to yourself to model each day the specific skills you want your child to display. For example, if your child's skill goals are kindness toward others, cooperative attitude, and respectful talk, list these specific behaviors as the ones you will model *frequently* to help your child learn these skills.

5. *The practice column*—In the practice column list "*all family interaction*" as a reminder to yourself that in all family interaction you have numerous opportunities to work on, practice, and model the high-priority skills you want your child to learn.

6. *The other methods of influence column*—In this column list several other positive methods of influence that may help your child learn his high-priority skills more rapidly. For example, you could list the nightly review technique, the technique of proudly discussing your child's progress with his other parent, the technique of removing aggressive or violent television, and

command–compliance training. Sometimes parents add additional techniques such as reading or viewing children's stories and videos that contain kindness themes or themes of cooperation, sharing, telling the truth, and so forth (Strayhorn 1988).

Guidelines for Using the High-Priority Skills Workplan

1. Once you have selected your child's goals, review with him the specific skills you want him to practice each day. Establishing clear goals for your child will help him know the specific behaviors and attitudes you want him to display more frequently. At the end of this discussion post your child's goals in his room using a form like the one in Table 7–2 in Chapter 7.

2. Post the entire skills workplan where you are likely to see it every day as a cue to keep yourself focused on *all* of the plan's components. Once a week review the entire plan to keep yourself firmly on track.

3. At least once a week provide feedback to your child's other parent on how well he/she is following the plan and ask him/her to give you feedback on how you are doing. Don't get defensive if you receive criticism. Use the criticism to correct your behavior so that you can *forcefully* and *consistently* implement the methods of influence listed on the workplan.

6
Building
Thinking Skills

Behavior modification methods are effective in promoting better functioning in oppositional children. However, total reliance on external behavior modification techniques runs the risk of training your child to think his behavior can be controlled only by external forces. The goal of this chapter is to teach you the common forms of irrational thinking that contribute to some of your child's inappropriate behaviors and attitudes. This section will also provide you with a repertoire of rational (helpful) ideas that you can teach your child to use when provoked, teased, challenged, or frustrated.

The more often your child can think rationally about day-to-day problems and frustrations, the greater the chance he will display more appropriate behaviors, attitudes, and feelings. He may also begin to understand that his behavior can be controlled from within, by the process of thinking more rationally about social problems and frustrations.

Before you begin working with your child to help straighten out his thinking, be sure that your thinking is "straight" as well. You might want to review Chapter 2 again; if you are ready for more extensive help, read one of the adult self-help books on rational approaches to life listed at the end of this book.

The remainder of this chapter is based upon the work of Albert Ellis (1994), the founder of Rational-Emotive

Behavior Therapy (REBT), and Bernard and Joyce (1984), who have applied REBT principles to clinical work with children and adolescents. This section covers the irrational beliefs that create some of your oppositional child's main behavioral problems, an analysis of why these beliefs are irrational, and the desired alternative rational beliefs that will help your child cope more adaptively and display better behaviors and attitudes.

Before you begin teaching your child rational thinking skills, a couple of points on teaching technique are in order. Teach your child to think rationally when he is calm, or gently offer a rational coping statement as a cue to your child when a problem is developing. When your child begins to use rational thinking to calm down or control behavior, be sure to provide "enthusiastic attention" to his newly emerging thinking skills. If your child has lost control and is very upset or angry, do not coach him with rational thinking at that point because he may develop resistance to rational thinking just to spite you. Rather, wait until the storm has passed and then, as needed, gently begin to reintroduce rational thinking. A final point—it will take much *practice* and *repetition* to help your child develop good thinking skills.

THE IRRATIONAL BELIEFS OF OPPOSITIONAL/ DEFIANT CHILDREN

The material in this section is not an all-inclusive review of the oppositional child's symptoms and irrational beliefs. It is, however, a look at some of the common symptoms and irrational beliefs that oppositional/defiant children display and utilize frequently. Carefully review the following eight problem areas and the corresponding "thinking remedies" so you can begin to teach your child how to think rationally. The sections on anger, cheating, lying, and stealing are brief summaries of more extensive discussions of these problems by Bernard and Joyce (1984).

1. *Irrational beliefs associated with hating, damning anger*—Hating, damning anger occurs when your child believes: "Because I don't like what you are doing you *must* not do it." "Because you did that *horrible* act you are a *total* rat who deserves severe punishment." "You've got no right to treat me in this unfair way."

Analysis—This type of thinking by your child is irrational because there is no law of the universe that says others must behave in the way your child demands; your child has irrationally rated another person's behavior as horrible—110 percent bad—worse than the worst thing that could ever happen to him, which it is not; your child has totally "trashed" another person as *all bad*, which is a distortion of reality; and your child is demanding that the world be fair when often it isn't.

Rational alternative beliefs—To reduce hating, damning anger, teach your child to think: "I dislike your behavior but *tough*, that's the way you sometimes act." "It's a hassle that you treat me badly, but there are worse problems that could happen to a kid." "Like all kids you [the other kid] sometimes act badly but you are never an all bad person." "I *wish* the world was fair but many times it isn't. Tough! I can handle it."

2. *Irrational beliefs behind a defiant attitude toward adults*—A defiant attitude toward adults emerges when your child believes: "To feel worthwhile and powerful I *must* tell you off," and "By talking back to grownups I will really prove that I rate as a person and have power."

Analysis—Thinking like this is irrational because your child believes that his value as a person *and* his personal power are enhanced by acting in a provocative and defiant manner. He believes that self-worth is tied to behavior, good or bad, when logically it is not; and personal power is evident only through a direct verbal assault on authority figures.

Rational alternative beliefs—To reduce a defiant attitude, suggest the following ideas to your child. "I am always an okay, worthwhile kid, so I don't need to prove it by talking back," and "Words and ideas spoken in a nice tone of voice have power too."

3. *Irrational belief associated with oppositional behavior*—Oppositional behavior emerges when your child believes: "To prove that I am in *control*, I *must* *resist* directions and requests from grownups."

Analysis—Although oppositional/noncompliant behavior is in many ways learned behavior, it often reflects the child's desire to demonstrate control over an adult. The irrational demand that the child places on him- or herself in this situation is a demand to resist at almost all costs. Also, the child irrationally believes that control is demonstrated only through resistance, when in fact control may be expressed in many other more adaptive ways.

Rational alternative belief—To help eliminate oppositional behavior, teach your child to think: "I am enough in control to show that I can cooperate and even do things I don't like to do."

4. *Irrational beliefs associated with lying*—Lying occurs when your child thinks: "To feel good about myself, I *must* behave *perfectly*. If I mess up, I'm worthless and deserve punishment." "I cannot risk feeling worthless or getting punished, so I will lie about what I did."

Analysis—Again, your child is irrationally linking self-worth to isolated behaviors and for this reason believes that lying will protect his fragile self-esteem. (Be aware, however, that lying is rational if a child has been receiving a great deal of harsh punishment. It is rational and self-protective to try to avoid severe punishment.)

Rational alternative beliefs—To reduce lying, suggest the following ideas: "I messed up like all kids sometimes do, but I'm still okay and worthwhile as a person." "I'll admit that I acted badly, but I won't put myself down. Sometimes I make mistakes." "I am tough enough to tell the truth. If I do get punished, I can handle it."

5. *Irrational beliefs associated with cheating*—

Cheating occurs when a child believes: "I am a *total* failure as a kid when I fail at something." "Failing is *terrible*. I can't handle the shame of not doing well, so I'll cheat to make myself look good."

Analysis—This type of thinking is irrational. To be a total failure, a child would have to fail continuously at everything from dawn to dusk, 365 days a year, which no child ever does. Failing at things, making mistakes, and not doing well, though unpleasant, are not horrible, terrible, and awful events. Failing at something is far from the worst thing that could ever happen to a child.

Rational alternative beliefs—To help eliminate cheating, encourage the use of the following ideas: "Like all other kids, I will sometimes win and sometimes lose, but I am always worthwhile." "Although it's a hassle to lose and it feels unpleasant, there are worse things that could happen to a kid. I can handle it."

6. *Irrational beliefs associated with stealing*—Stealing occurs when your child believes: "I'm not getting the kind of approval that I *demand*, so I'm going to steal anything I want to make myself feel better." "I must always get my fair share of 'goodies' in this unfair world." "I can't stand it [i.e., *I'll die*] if others have more than I have."

Analysis—This type of thinking is not reality based because the child irrationally believes that self-worth is improved by taking things, or that taking things is an adequate substitute for parental approval, when clearly it is not. He also believes the world must be fair even though often it is not, and death will occur if he can't have as much as others have.

Rational alternative beliefs—To help your child stop stealing, promote the following ideas: "I am a worthwhile person whether or not I am getting approval and attention from others." "I'll likely never have as much as some people have. Tough! That's the way it is in this world." "I'll *live* if others have more than me and *I can still have fun*."

7. *Irrational beliefs associated with low frustration tolerance*—Low frustration tolerance occurs when a child believes: "I must always get what I want *immediately* and *easily*"; "Adults must never make me do things I don't want to do"; "It's horrible when I can't get what I want"; "I can't stand not getting what I want or getting what I don't want."

Analysis—These beliefs are irrational because your child believes that demanding that things be easy will make it happen that way, even though much of what we obtain or acquire in life requires effort and hard work. He believes he has the Godlike power to determine the workings of the world, even though frequently the world dishes out things we don't want but have to cope with nonetheless. He feels it is a horror not to get what one wants immediately (when clearly it is not), and that death, fainting, or paralysis will occur when he does not get what he wants or when he gets something that he doesn't want.

Rational alternative beliefs—To improve frustration tolerance, suggest the following ideas: "Although I would like to get what I want easily, I'm probably going to have to work hard and tolerate uncomfortable feelings to get what I want. It's a pain that I can't get what I want or have to deal with things that I don't want, but it's not a disaster. I *can* handle it when I can't get what I want or have to deal with something that I don't want. I'll live."

8. *Irrational beliefs associated with property destruction/physical aggression*—Property destruction and physical aggression may occur when your child believes: "My personal worth is destroyed if you mess with me in any way, so I will destroy you [*you piece of trash*] or your property to make you hurt *real* bad."

Analysis—This is extremely irrational thinking because your child believes that his self-esteem depends on what another person says or does, when it does not. He also believes another person is *all* bad, which is not possible, that hateful, destructive revenge can restore self-worth or self-esteem, which it cannot, and that forgiveness toward others is not possible, when it is.

Rational alternative beliefs—To reduce aggression toward others, offer the following ideas: "I am always worthwhile and okay, even when someone else gets in my way or treats me disrespectfully or unfairly. There are no all-bad people, only people who sometimes act badly." In addition: "I am already a worthwhile kid, so I don't have to hurt others or their belongings to know that I am okay, and I *can* forgive people for treating me badly."

Encourage your child to use these coping statements frequently. As he begins to apply his new thinking skills when provoked, teased, or frustrated, he will be better able to moderate feelings and behaviors, solve day-to-day problems, stay out of trouble, and have more fun.

7
Monitoring Progress

An ongoing plan to monitor your child's progress will help him maintain his behavioral improvement. In this final chapter you will learn how to help your child monitor his progress and take responsibility for inappropriate behaviors. I will also offer a few final tips to keep in mind for future use.

ENCOURAGING ACCURATE SELF-REFLECTION

Children who display oppositional, defiant, and aggressive behavior frequently blame others for their problems and deny or minimize their own behavioral difficulties. This tendency to externalize responsibility for problems is generally a source of great frustration for parents, because the child acts as if he has no responsibility for his inappropriate actions. Out of frustration, parents, sometimes resort to lectures, interrogations, yelling, and a variety of other coercive methods to browbeat the child into admitting mistakes and taking responsibility for his bad behavior. Such methods generally backfire and instead push the child to blame others even more, especially the angry, accusing parents.

To help a defiant child learn to take responsibility for his actions and develop the capacity for self-reflection, a gentler method is needed. A less confrontational approach will reduce the chances of your child becoming angry and defensive and will create a more positive atmosphere within which all behavior can be examined and understood. The method I recommend to promote self-reflection in defiant children is a modified version of a psychotherapy technique designed to help impulsive children develop the skill of accurate self-evaluation (Kendall and Braswell 1993).

To monitor your child's progress on his daily goals and help him develop the capacity for self-reflection, use the following method.

1. Take a few minutes at the end of each day to compare notes with your child on how well he practiced his high-priority skills that day. Before you meet with your child complete a parent report form like the one displayed in Table 7–1. As you rate your child's progress on each of his goals, be sure to note the specific behavioral evidence you are using as the basis of your rating.

2. During your meeting with your child, calmly and supportively ask him to review his goals and then, using a child self-report form like the one displayed in Table 7–2, ask him to circle and discuss the rating that best describes his behavior that day in relation to each specific goal. (If your child cannot yet read, omit the forms and follow these guidelines using a discussion format only.)

Table 7–1.   Parent Report

How did my child do today?   Today's Date _____

My child's skill-goals are:

1. ____ Kind and gentle with others ____
2. ____ Good sport when frustrated ____
3. ____ Follow directions/cooperative attitude ____
4. ____ Respectful talk ____

Today on Goal ① he/she did → very well — OK — not so hot
(Evidence? _____)

Today on Goal ② he/she did → very well — OK — not so hot
(Evidence? _____)

Today on Goal ③ he/she did → very well — OK — not so hot
(Evidence? _____)

Today on Goal ④ he/she did → very well — OK — not so hot
(Evidence? _____)

1. If any portion of your child's self-report matches any of your ratings of his goals (whether he did well or poorly), praise him for giving an accurate report on that goal or goals.

2. If your child gives an inaccurate self-report (e.g., he claims good behavior on a day when many problems occurred), gently encourage him to think again about what happened today. If your child does not come up with an accurate report, provide him with your feedback. Then tell your child that tomorrow you and he will have another chance to compare notes on his behavior.

3. For any problem area rated "OK" or "not so hot," discuss with your child an adaptive problem-solving plan that he can use tomorrow should the same difficult situation occur.

4. Remember, do not criticize, blame, or lecture your child during the self-reflection discussion.

3. Next, share your report with your child. Remember, provide feedback in a supportive manner: "Chris, I agree with your report. I think you did very well practicing kindness today because I saw you help your sister when she fell down and scraped her knee." Or, "Chris, I agree. Today it looked to me like you were not very kind to your sister because when she fell down and scraped her knee you laughed at her."

4. If any portion of your child's self-report matches any of your ratings of his goals, praise him for giving an accurate report on that goal or goals. For example,

Table 7–2.   Child Self-Report

How did I do today?   Today's Date _____

My goals are:

1. ____ Kind and gentle with others
2. ____ Good sport when frustrated
3. ____ Follow directions/cooperative attitude
4. ____ Respectful talk

Today on Goal ① I did → very well — okay — not so hot
Today on Goal ② I did → very well — okay — not so hot
Today on Goal ③ I did → very well — okay — not so hot
Today on Goal ④ I did → very well — okay — not so hot

1. If you did pretty well on your goals today, pat yourself on the back and tell yourself: "I did a good job today!"

2. If you had a hard day today, talk to your parents about how you can stay out of trouble and make tomorrow a better day.

3. Remember, even if you had problems today, you are always a good person.

if your child acknowledges that he was not kind to others today, praise him for truthfully reporting on his behavior: "Chris, you did a good job telling me that you were not kind to your sister today. I'm very proud of you for giving a truthful report."

5. If your child gives an inaccurate self-report (e.g., he claims good behavior on a day when many problems occurred), gently encourage him to think again about his behavior. If he does not produce an accurate report, provide him with your feedback. Then tell your child that tomorrow will bring another chance to compare notes on his behavior: "Okay, Chris, I guess you and I see things differently today. I think you were not kind to your sister because you kept calling her nasty names. I hope that tomorrow you will try harder to be kind to her. Tomorrow after dinner we'll review your goals again."

6. Remember, do not criticize, blame, scold, or lecture your child during the self-reflection discussion.

7. For any problem area that you and your child both rate as "okay" or "not so hot," discuss an adaptive problem-solving plan that he can use tomorrow should the same difficult situation occur again.

Over time, this supportive technique may help your child begin to reflect and accurately report on his behavior, both good and bad. It will probably take much repetition of this particular method to show results. Do not be discouraged if your child does not give accurate self-reports right away.

A FEW FINAL TIPS

To sustain your child's behavioral recovery keep the following points in mind.

1. For some oppositional, defiant, and aggressive children the path toward recovery is characterized by alternating phases of improvement and brief flare-ups of disruptive behavior. In other words, progress usually occurs in a "two steps forward, one step backward" format. Do not be discouraged when this happens. Just keep using the techniques you have learned in this book. Over time, the flare-ups of disruptive behavior displayed by your child should occur less frequently.

2. As time goes by some parents start to forget about their child management plan or drift away from the use of positive social reinforcement for good behavior and penalties for bad behavior. At least once a month ask yourself: "Am I *consistently* using all of the methods of influence I have learned to help my child learn new behaviors and attitudes?" If your answer is no, reread this book. If your answer is yes, take yourself and a friend out to dinner.

3. Keep your child management plan in place when you are on vacation and during the summertime.

4. Remember, keep your anger under control, be playful with your child, remain optimistic about his future, and find ways to get out of the house and have some fun for yourself. There really is more to life than just raising children.

CONCLUSION

Parents are in control of many methods of influence to help an oppositional/defiant child learn new behaviors, attitudes, and ways of thinking about day-to-day problems. If you use the method described in this book consistently for 12 weeks, you will probably see substantial improvement in your child's behavior. If not, consult a child mental health professional for additional help, and do not lose hope. Finally, as you work with your child each day keep the following idea in mind: *"A diamond is just a piece of coal that stuck to its job."* I hope all goes well for you and your child.

APPENDIX
Guidelines
for Clinicians

Although this book may be used by parents as a self-help resource, it was also designed to be a parent training manual for clinicians. Therapists specializing in the treatment of children, particularly children with disruptive behavior disorders, will find the approach I have developed to be a helpful first stage of intervention for many oppositional, defiant, and aggressive children. Because the text of this manual can be easily read by parents, it also supports a focused collaboration between parents and therapists toward a common goal—the rapid behavioral recovery of a defiant/aggressive child.

Before I discuss aspects of technique related to each of the seven chapters or stages of this intervention, I will offer a few general comments and guidelines for clinicians.

1. This parent training intervention is indicated for any 4- to 10-year-old child diagnosed with an externalizing or disruptive behavior disorder. It is contraindicated in cases in which a child's parent has a mental illness, substance abuse problem, or marital problem so severe that it would prevent the parent from learning and applying the skills described. In such situations these problems should be treated first.

2. The book supports a *skills-based* treatment for parents. It was written specifically to help parents acquire and maintain new methods of influence to promote social, behavioral, and attitudinal competence in their children.

3. To help parents learn new skills faster and use them longer, that is, further into the future, the concurrent use of readings, discussion, homework, in-session role play, and videos is recommended.

4. When parents are being trained in child management methods, it is helpful for the therapist to define his or her role as teacher, consultant, philosopher, and coach.

5. It is generally advisable for clinicians to remain focused initially on behavioral improvement and stabilization for the child. Behavioral improvement usually helps children feel substantially better, and it goes a long way toward improving the quality of the parent–child relationship.

6. Once the child has started to display improved behavior, clinicians, in consultation with parents, can decide whether additional treatment is needed to address other family or intrapsychic issues that may be affecting the child adversely.

7. The method detailed in this book can be used in conjunction with any type of individual psychotherapy that is being provided to the child, for example, cognitive–behavioral psychotherapy, psychodynamic psychotherapy, or psychoanalysis.

8. This parent training intervention can be conducted with parents individually or in a parent training group format.

9. The effectiveness of this intervention will be influenced by a number of variables, including the degree to which parents are able to learn new child management skills, the nature and severity of the child's disorder, and the nature and severity of disturbance in a parent.

My initial start-to-finish involvement with a child who has a disruptive behavior disorder typically lasts 8 to 12 weeks and is divided into five distinct phases, described below. Phases two through four can be lengthened or shortened as dictated by the parents' progress in mastering new child management skills and by the response of the child to the parent training intervention. The phases are *Diagnostic Evaluation* (one to two sessions), *Getting Ready for Change* (one to three sessions), *Par-*

ent Training in Child Management Methods (three to
five sessions), *Introducing the Child to Rational Thinking* (two to three sessions), and *Aftercare Phase* (booster
sessions as needed). These five phases capture the
basic structure of my approach.

Questions sometimes arise about what to tell a child
about a parent training intervention. After I have evalu-
ated a child and determined that he or she might benefit from the method described in this book, I meet with
the parents to share the results of my evaluation and
my recommendation for a parent training intervention.
If the parents agree to this recommendation, I tell the
child that I enjoyed meeting him, that I can see that he
is a boy (or girl) who very much wants to do well, and
that his parents and I will try to help him do better. I
also tell the child that I will not be seeing him for a
month or two, but that I will be meeting with his parents to think about ways to help him solve his problems. I have found that most children are quite accept-
ing of this arrangement, and when they return to sessions
some 6 to 8 weeks later they generally have no problem relating to me or engaging in the treatment.

I will now offer a few points on technique related
to the seven chapters of this book. Typically I ask parents to read the chapter associated with the training
before attending the relevant training session. Sessions
begin with a review of the parents' comprehension of
the concepts and techniques to be covered that week.
Based on this assessment I make immediate judgments

about how to shape the training session to best meet each parent's individual learning needs or to deal with irrational beliefs and emotional blocks related to the use of specific child management strategies.

Chapter 1—*Getting Ready for Change*: After parents read this first section I use Table 1–1, the "Parent Preflight Checklist," to structure the session. As parents review this list of topics, I ask which areas, if any, they believe they need to work on to improve the chances that the child management techniques they will learn in later chapters will be effective. This usually leads to a straightforward discussion of individual factors that will help or hinder efforts to change and to promote improved behavior in the child.

Once a parent has identified a problem area(s), for example, anger control, procrastination, hectic week problem, the focus shifts to strategies to eliminate such obstacles to change. It is important to note that the problems identified for improvement do not need to be solved in their entirety to move forward. As long as a parent is able to demonstrate some improvement in the designated area(s), it is reasonable to move on to subsequent stages of this intervention. It is advisable, however, to arrange with the parent(s) a periodic review of progress overcoming the problems they have identified as barriers to change.

Chapter 2—*What Is Your Parenting Philosophy?*: At this stage I use Figure 2–1, "Rational and Irrational Parenting Attitudes," to focus the discussion. I ask parents to review this chart, disclose their specific areas of irrational thinking, and then work on ways to eliminate such attitudes/beliefs. I also review the advantages of adhering to a rational parenting philosophy and the disadvantages of clinging to irrational beliefs about an oppositional child.

It is important to convey to parents that they are not to strive for perfection in ridding themselves of irrational beliefs, because no human being is ever totally free from irrational thinking, self-defeating emotions, and dysfunctional behaviors. Rational thinking (and the more moderate emotions and behaviors that flow from such thinking) is a goal to be pursued continuously but not perfectionistically. As long as a parent is operating primarily within a framework of rational thought, the chances of helping a child function better are improved. To help parents internalize rational parenting beliefs, a *daily* review of the coping statements listed at the end of this chapter should be encouraged.

Chapter 3—*Winning Cooperation from Your Child*: At this stage I begin formal parent training in child management methods. One of the main goals of this phase is to introduce parents to the skill of differential attention (Forehand and McMahon 1981), that is, responding enthusiastically to good, appropriate, competent behavior and thinking in the child, and ignoring bad, inappropriate, incompetent behavior and thinking as much as possible. This chapter teaches parents a variety of positive reinforcement techniques to encourage cooperative behavior from the child. To support skill development in this area, I often show parents a 25-minute video entitled "The Art of Effective Praising" (Webster-Stratton 1984), which illustrates the multifaceted nature of good praising technique.

At this point parents are also helped to review the overall emotional and behavioral tone of their home, start using all of the positive social reinforcement techniques discussed in this chapter, and structure the child's day so that chores and tasks are completed before access to daily privileges is allowed.

Chapter 4—*Penalties for Noncompliance, Defiance, and Aggression*: In this step there is further discussion of the skill of differential attention, mainly as it pertains to ignoring inappropriate behaviors. Once parents grasp the essential elements of ignoring, I move on to train them in the three variations of the time-out procedure discussed in this chapter. The use of Figure 4–1, "The Parental Command–Consequence Procedure," facilitates learning of the time-out technique. At this point I also often show an 18-minute video entitled "Limit Setting" (Kavanagh et al. 1991), which shows examples of parents setting limits, using time-out, and following through on consequences. Before parents use penalty techniques, it is important for them to review the penalty skills ground rules detailed in this chapter.

Chapter 5—*Building Social and Behavioral Skills*: This short chapter is used to help parents identify specific social and behavioral goals for the child and, through the use of the high-priority skills workplan, to map out the multiple methods of influence that will be used to help the child develop more competent behaviors, social skills, and attitudes. At this point I often use a session to write the skills workplan collaboratively with parents and to reinforce the need for parents to use the plan vigorously and consistently. At the end of this session (or phase) it is generally time to prepare for the child's return to sessions and to clarify that the parents' role in such sessions will be to observe, and if necessary take notes on, the talks I have with the child.

Chapter 6—*Building Thinking Skills*: At this point I invite the child back to the sessions and begin to introduce him or her to rational thinking. For children 7 to 10 years of age I am usually able to help them see to some extent why their irrational beliefs are irrational (unhelpful). I also am able, by means of the techniques described by Bernard and Joyce (1984), to encourage many children to begin using rational coping statements to develop "psychological armor" against life's insults and provocations. For younger children 4 to 6 years of age I simply teach them to repeat simple coping statements when they are frustrated and praise them when they do so. There are a number of children in my caseload running around town practicing "I can handle it," "It could be worse," "I'm a worthwhile kid" types of thoughts to their benefit.

During this phase parents are present as I conduct individual psychotherapy with the child. The parents listen to my dialogue with the child so they can learn how to coach him or her in the use of rational thinking at home. The presence of the parents encourages them to become my "agents of skill generalization," and they become able to help the child use better thinking skills outside of sessions. Chapter 6 was written for parents to use as a quick reference guide to rational thinking for defiant children.

Chapter 7—*Monitoring Progress*: This chapter presents a structured method for monitoring the child's progress. The main technique discussed is a parental monitoring procedure that simultaneously reinforces the child's social and behavioral goals, helps the child develop the capacity for accurate self-reflection, and provides a forum for parent and child to discuss solutions to problems. Once implemented, this daily monitoring exercise between parent and child becomes the centerpiece of the child's aftercare plan. At this point I often initiate termination with the understanding that the parents will continue to work with the child's teacher and other involved professionals as long as necessary to manage the child's recovery. Parents are advised to call me for booster sessions as needed.

This parent training intervention does not always produce the desired outcome. Unfortunately, some children remain embedded in oppositional, defiant, and aggressive modes of relatedness. In these cases I first consider the possibility of longer term outpatient treatment for the child and his family. If further outpatient treatment is not advisable, I usually recommend referral to a more structured level of care, such as a day treatment or residential treatment program.

There is nothing absolute or dogmatic in these guidelines. Clinicians should feel free to adapt or modify any aspect of my approach based upon their clinical judgment and the individual treatment needs of each child and his parents. Nevertheless, for a substantial number of children who present with disruptive behavior disorders, the parent training method described in this book generally—though not always—yields rapid behavioral improvement for the child and a positive therapeutic experience for the entire family.

Suggested Reading

Procrastination

Bernard, M. (1991). *Procrastinate Later!* Melbourne: Schwartz and Wilkinson.

This book presents Dr. Bernard's magnetic theory of procrastination. This theory is based on nine major factors that push or repel you away from hard tasks and one key factor that pulls or draws you away from the work that you need to do. Dr. Bernard also discusses, in considerable detail, the various addictions, fantasies, and self-lies that produce procrastination. This book will provide you with insight into the psychology of procrastination, as well as twenty-five specific self-help techniques to overcome it.

Ellis, A., and Knaus, W. (1977). *Overcoming Procrastination.* New York: New American Library.

This book does a remarkable job of examining psychological factors that can produce the behavior known as procrastination. In their discussion, Drs. Ellis and Knaus show how self-downing, low frustration tolerance, hostility, perfectionism, anxiety, guilt, shame, or depression may lead to avoidance of tasks and responsibilities. This book also illuminates many of the irrational beliefs that contribute to procrastination. If your procrastination does not prevent you from finishing this book, you will learn a variety of cognitive, emotive, and behavioral techniques to overcome the problems noted above and increase your work productivity at home and at the office.

Anger Management

Barrish, H., and Barrish, I. J. (1989). *Managing and Understanding Parental Anger.* Kansas City: Westport.

This is a great book and the one I most often recommend to parents to reduce and prevent overly angry responses to their children. In a clear and concise manner the authors teach parents the major unhelpful beliefs that create intense anger toward children and offer specific thinking remedies designed to lower anger. Although it is only forty-three pages in length, you will find this book packed with advice that will help improve the quality of your relationship with your child.

Ellis, A. (1977). *Anger: How to Live With and Without it.* Secaucus, NJ: Citadel.

When it comes to a discussion of anger, this book leaves no stone unturned. Throughout his discussion Dr. Ellis systematically shows how you create and maintain your anger by holding rigidly to self-angering philosophies about other people and the world. This book will help you detect and dispute your self-angering philosophies and beliefs, and it will teach you numerous ways to think, feel, and act your way out of an overly angry outlook on life.

Hauck, P. A. (1974). *Overcoming Frustration and Anger.* Philadelphia: Westminster. (Now available through Westminster/John Knox in Louisville, KY.)

This is another good book to help you learn about the sources of your anger and to change yourself into a less angry person. In the discussion Dr. Hauck shows you the complete psychological sequence of getting angry. He also shows how to deal with self-righteous anger and how to stop being so blaming of others. The book concludes with nine specific guidelines for overcoming frustration and anger.

Rational Living and Parenting

Ellis, A. (1988). *How to Stubbornly Refuse to Make Yourself Miserable About Anything—Yes, Anything!* Secaucus, NJ: Lyle Stuart.

This is a book you should stubbornly refuse to put down until you have finished it. It will give you many insights into the ways in which you needlessly disturb yourself over a variety of life problems. The self-help techniques it contains will also help you gain control of your emotional destiny so that you can maximally enjoy life and have as little emotional pain as possible.

Ellis, A., and Harper, R. A. (1975). *A New Guide to Rational Living*. North Hollywood, CA: Wilshire.

This guide to rational living is one of the most widely read self-help books in the world. In it Drs. Ellis and Harper discuss in detail ten irrational beliefs that cause human psychological disturbance. If you study this book carefully and actively model its self-helping philosophies around your child, you will be giving him or her a great head start in knowing how not to become an emotionally disturbed individual.

Hauck, P. (1967). *The Rational Management of Children*. Roslyn Heights, NY: Libra. (Now available through Libra in San Diego, CA.)

This book will teach you many ways to promote psychological health in your child. Dr. Hauck discusses the common erroneous beliefs about child management, as well as specific guidelines to help children conquer fears of failure and fears of rejection and ridicule. He also discusses ways that you can help your child overcome states of anger and depression and offers sound advice on methods of discipline.

Hauck, P. (1971). *Overcoming The Rating Game*. Louisville, KY: Westminster/John Knox.

If you want to learn how to recognize the signs of low self-esteem and overcome feelings of inferiority, this is the book for you. Once learned, Dr. Hauck's philosophy of unconditional self-acceptance will give you the ability to never put yourself down, even though you may fail at many things in life, as most people do. By living a philosophy of unconditional self-acceptance, you will also model for your child an approach to self and others that promotes and sustains psychological well-being.

Dawson, P. (1994). *Homework Survival Guide: Parent Handout*. North Tonowanda, NY: Multi-Health Systems.

This short pamphlet teaches you just about all you need to know to help your child improve his or her homework performance. I frequently give this survival guide to parents, who find Dr. Dawson's method easy to use and effective.

References

Barkley, R. (1987). *Defiant Children: A Clinician's Manual for Parent Training.* New York: Guilford.

Bernard, M., and Joyce, M. (1984). *Rational-Emotive Therapy with Children and Adolescents.* New York: Wiley.

Breen, M., and Altepeter, T. (1990). *Disruptive Behavior Disorders in Children.* New York: Guilford.

Chess, S., and Thomas, A. (1991). Temperament. In *Child and Adolescent Psychiatry: A Comprehensive Textbook,* ed. M. Lewis, pp. 145–159. Baltimore: Williams & Wilkins.

Ellis, A. (1975). *How to Live with a Neurotic.* Hollywood, CA: Wilshire.

——— (1994). *Reason and Emotion in Psychotherapy.* New York: Birch Lane.

Ellis, A., and Dryden, W. (1987). *The Practice of Rational Emotive Therapy.* New York: Springer.

Forehand, R., and McMahon, R. (1981). *Helping the Noncompliant Child*. New York: Guilford.

Huber, C., and Baruth, L. (1989). *Rational-Emotive Family Therapy*. New York: Springer.

Kavanagh, K., Frey, J., and Larsen, D. (producers) (1991). *Growing Opportunities School-Age Series Part 2: Limit Setting* (videotape). Eugene, OR: Castalia.

Kazdin, A. (1994). *Behavior Modification in Applied Settings*, 5th ed. Pacific Grove, CA: Brooks/Cole.

Kendall, P., and Braswell, L. (1993). *Cognitive-Behavioral Therapy for Impulsive Children*, 2nd ed. New York: Guilford.

King, R., and Noshpitz, J. (1991). Conduct disorder. In *Pathways of Growth: Essentials of Child Psychiatry*, vol. 2: *Psychopathology*, pp. 400–452. New York: Wiley.

Lewis, D. (1991). Conduct disorder. In *Child and Adolescent Psychiatry: A Comprehensive Textbook*, ed. M. Lewis, pp. 561–573. Baltimore: Williams & Wilkins.

Porter-Thal, N. (1994). *Parents, Children and Divorce*, 4th ed. Fort Meyers, FL: The Training Company.

Strayhorn, J. (1988). *The Competent Child*. New York: Guilford.

Webster-Stratton, C. (producer) (1984). *The Parents and Children Series Praise and Rewards Program Part I: The Art of Effective Praising* (videotape). Eugene, OR: Castalia.

Index

ABOUT THE AUTHOR

Kenneth Wenning received his MSW (1980) and Ph.D. (1988) from the Smith College School for Social Work in Northampton, Massachusetts. For the past fifteen years he has specialized in the evaluation and treatment of children who are oppositional, defiant, and aggressive. Currently he works in New Haven at the Clifford W. Beers Guidance Clinic where he teaches, supervises, and conducts research. Dr. Wenning also maintains a private practice of child and family treatment in Hamden, Connecticut.